THE NEWS
THE EVENTS
AND
THE LIVES
OF 1974

Elizabeth Absalom & Pauline Watson

D'Azur Publishing

Second Edition

Published by D'Azur Publishing 2023
D'Azur Publishing is a Division of D'Azur Limited

Copyright © D'Azur Publishing 2023
Pauline Watson has asserted her right under the Copyright, Design and Patents Act 1988 to be identified as the author of this work.

The language, phrases and terminology within this book are as written at the time of the news reports during the year covered and convey and illustrate the sentiments at that time, even though modern society may find some words inappropriate. The news reports are taken from internationally recognised major newspapers and other sources of the year in question. The language does not represent any personal view of the author or publisher.

All Rights Reserved. No part of this publication may be reproduced, stored or transmitted in any form or by any means, electronic, mechanical, digital or otherwise, except under the terms of the Copyright, Designs and Patents Act 1988 or under terms of a licence issued by the publisher. This book is sold subject to the condition that it shall not, by way of trade or otherwise, be lent, resold or hired out, or otherwise circulated without the publishers prior consent in any form or binding or cover other than that in which it is published and without a similar condition, including this condition, being imposed on the subsequent purchaser.
All requests to the Publisher for permission should be addressed to info@d-azur.com.

First published in Great Britain in 2023 by D'Azur Limited
Second Edition Published 2024
Contact: info@d-azur.com Visit www.d-azur.com
ISBN 9798875772801

ACKNOWLEDGEMENTS
The publisher wishes to acknowledge the following people and sources:

British Newspaper Archive; The Times Archive; Cover Malcolm Watson; p6 Forrexp - Own work; p10 Prioryman - Own work; p11 Rudolf Stricker; p12 Bechtel Corporation; Alsi; p14 (Sizewell) John Brodrick of the greenhousetrus; p17 Homage.com; p18 Malcolm Watson; p19 pasja1000; p21 (cube) Booyabazooka; Encik Tekateki - Own work(cube parts); Angelo_Giordano (Quake);p22 (Hippie) Strvnge Films; p23 Photo (Food) by Monique on Unsplash;25 Marcus_Fenix1; DeanG; NoGoodPizza; Michael D; p29 thip/media; xuyjs; p33 Greace Xaveria on Unsplash; Abe Books; ebay; p37 Moonpig; p39 Badiou Alain - Own work;p41 The Star; Robin Myerscough - Flickr; p43 Landmark Trust; Andree Stephan - Own work; 45 Image by Alain Audet from Pixabay; p47 Photo by Ijaz Rafi on Unsplash; p49 pompeytoffee22; Rept0n1x - Own work; Henry Tapper; p51 IBBY; p53 Malcolm Watson; p55 @nazanin; p57 Find My Past; Metropolitan Police; p59 Randwick Wap; Paul Barnett; p61 laurent marx from Pixabay; p63 Michael Schofield on Unsplash; mdgrafik0 from Pixabay; p63 Malcolm Watson; p53 The Sale room (coins); Wehwalt (service); p67 Malcolm Watson; p73 Philip Allfrey; Sodacan - Own work; p75 Matt Brown (New Market); EGFocus (flowers); Valeontravel (modern); p77 Koen Suyk / Anefo; p79 Copyright House of Lords 2022;p85 Zslap - Own work;p87 Nightflyer (talk);p89 slideplayer; p95 sarniebill1; p99 Jonathan Lucas; p101 alexander williams - Own work; p103 Ffestiniog & Welsh Highland Railway; visitwales; p105 Ilo from Pixabay; Matthias Böckel; The Wine Society; p109 Artcollection.io; p115 Duboeuf.com; p119 the Glenn Christodoulou Collection; Image by Erich Westendarp; p121 hadevora; Miti; p123 Qubes Pictures; Ken Haines;

Whilst we have made every effort to contact copyright holders, should we have made any omission, please contact us so that we can make the appropriate acknowledgement.

CONTENTS

1974 Highlights Of The Year   4-5

1974 The Year You Were Born   6-7

1979 The Year You Were Five   8-9

1985 The Year You Were Eleven   10-11

1990 The Year You Were Sixteen   12-13

1995 The Year You Were Twenty One   14-15

1974 Sporting Events   16-17

1974 Cultural Events   18-19

1974 Science and Nature   20-21

1974 Lives Of Everyday People   22-23

THE YEAR DAY-BY-DAY   **24-127**

The 1974 calendar   128

1974 Highlights

Monarch: Queen Elizabeth II   Prime Minister: Ted Heath (Conservative) From March 4th Harold Wilson (Labour)

1974 was a year of change and unrest. There were two general elections and two different governments; various industrial actions and strikes for better wages; a state of emergency declared in Northern Ireland and a terrorist bombing campaign on the British mainland by the IRA which put everyone on alert.

It was a year when the rich or influential hit the headlines for all the wrong reasons - Lord Lucan went missing after a murder, John Stonehouse MP disappeared, and there was the Poulson Affair which had Reggie Maudling, The Chancellor of the Exchequer suspected of fraud. Ordinary folk put up with bread shortages, a 3-day working week and petrol rationing. There was a local government reorganisation that did away with bits of our traditional and best loved counties in favour of brave new metropolitan authorities. But on the plus side, New Year's Day became a public holiday, the first McDonald's opened in Woolwich, and 'Bagpuss' first appeared on children's television.

Power cuts in the 3 day week (above). Old county of Westmorland (below).

FAMOUS PEOPLE WHO WERE BORN IN 1974

12th Jan: Mel C - 'Sporty Spice', pop singer
13th Feb: Robbie Williams, singer-songwriter
25th Feb: Dominic Raab, politician
28th Apr Vernon Kay, TV and radio presenter
7th Jun: Bear Grylls, adventurer and TV star
14th Jul: Maxine Peake, actress
6th Sep: Tim Henman, Tennis player
9th Sep: Gok Wan, stylist
29th Oct: Michael Vaughan, cricketer
24th Nov: Stephen Merchant, comedy actor

FAMOUS PEOPLE WHO DIED IN 1974

29th Jan: H.E.Bates, novelist
31st Jan: Samuel Goldwyn, Polish-born American film studio executive
23rd Feb: Raymond Glendenning, broadcaster
24th May: Duke Ellington, American jazz pianist
4th Jul: Georgette Heyer, novelist
22nd Aug: Jacob Bronowski, mathematician
26th Aug: Charles Lindburgh, American aviator
9thOct: Oskar Schindler, German humanitarian
26 Dec: Jack Benny, American actor

Of The Year

JANUARY The Conservative government introduced a 3-Day working week as a measure to reduce the use of electricity during the period of industrial action by the nation's coal miners.

FEBRUARY A coach carrying off duty soldiers and their families is the target of an IRA bomb on the M62. Twelve people die of injuries sustained in the explosion.

MARCH The miners' strike comes to an end when their union accepts an improved pay deal offered by the Labour Government.

APRIL Katie Boyle hosts the 19th Eurovision Song Contest in Brighton. A Swedish group called 'Abba' win a resounding victory.

MAY The fully electrified Western Coast railway line from London to Glasgow is opened. The journey time is reduced by an hour, to 5 hours.

JUNE Jon Pertwee is replaced by Tom Baker in the lead role as 'The Doctor' in the popular television science fiction series, 'Dr. Who'.

JULY Bill Shankly retires after 15 years as manager of Liverpool Football Club, having trained them up from a 2nd division side to UEFA winners.

AUGUST Charles Lindbergh, the American who in 1927 became the first man to fly solo across the Atlantic, died aged 72.

SEPTEMBER The world's first interactive public service information service - CEEFAX - went live on BBC television.

OCTOBER The 2nd general election this year results in a narrow victory for the Labour party and Harold Wilson forms the new government.

NOVEMBER Two pubs in the centre of Birmingham, The Mulberry Bush and The Tavern in The Town, both packed with young people, were blown up by IRA bombs. There were 21 fatalities, and 182 people were injured.

DECEMBER Reduced speed limits were introduced on Britain's roads in an effort to reduce fuel consumption during the Arab oil embargo which followed the Yom Kippur War.

Films and Arts

The **47th Academy Awards** in Los Angeles marked the last year NBC aired the show before ABC took over the broadcasting. Coppola's **Godfather II** starring Al Pacino, won twice the number of Oscars that the first film had.

There were two disaster movies, **Earthquake** and **Towering Inferno** which proved very successful at the box office, and period films **The Great Gatsby** starring Robert Redford and **Murder on The Orient Express** with Albert Finney, suited all age groups.

Despite not being a high scorer in the awards, one of the most enduring films in the popularity stakes was **Blazing Saddles**, starring Lee Marvin.

Television Comedy series remained ever popular with new programmes such as **Porridge** starring Ronnie Barker as the lovable old lag and prison warder Fulton McKay.

The pilot programme of **The Muppet Show** failed initially to ignite American enthusiasm but was liked by Lew Grade and production by ATV began in England in this year, while the long running **Monty Python's Flying Circus** came to an end.

In the literary world, the first book of the **Tinker, Tailor, Soldier, Spy** trilogy by John le Carre was published, as was Stephen King's first novel, **Carrie**, a horror tale which would go on to be a film classic.

5

1974 The Year

Born in 1974, you were one of 56.2 million people living in Britain and your life expectancy *then* was 72.4 years. You were one of the 13.2 births per 1,000 population, and the chance of dying as a child from infectious diseases such as measles, mumps, whooping cough or rubella was diminishing thanks to Britain's robust childhood vaccination programme. However, some diseases such as tuberculosis and polio remained with us, largely due to increasing numbers of immigrants settling here from countries with poorer health security measures.

Growing unrest both here and abroad brought price rises and food shortages, and the general standard of living for many in Britain stagnated or fell. There was an increasing aspiration to 'social betterment' but for many in the poorer industrial areas this remained a dream.

1974 was a year of increasing discontent. The Yom Kippur War, although on the other side of the world had a disastrous effect on Britain, with unemployment and inflation spiralling. Immigration continued to rise, putting pressure on the job market and leading to increased racial unrest. People became used to bomb alerts as the IRA continued their terror campaign against British authority.

The fashion silhouette was smart and tailored with flared trousers, A-line skirts, belted jackets and polo neck jumpers.

Synthetic fibres were used more and more and natural fibres were 'out'. Chief among the new 'easy care' – 'easy wear' fabrics was Crimplene, which was available in an endless variety of designs and colours.

The continued influence of pop-culture coupled with television and advertising gave rise to trends. Edinburgh boy band 'The Bay City Rollers' started a 'run' on tartan fabric for the teen market, while Vivienne Westwood stocked her London boutique 'Sex' with as much plaid fashion as she could produce.

Soviet car manufacturer Lada, founded four years ago with Italian car giant Fiat, begins selling cars in the United Kingdom. The four-door saloon was based on the Fiat 124 and cost £999.

How Much Did It Cost?

The Average Pay	£1,981 (£38 pw)
The Average House	£10,000
Loaf of White Bread	14.5p
Pint of Milk	4.5p
Pint of Beer	22.5p
Gallon of Petrol	50p
Newspapers	3-5p
To Post a letter in UK	4.5p
12mnths Road Tax	£25
TV Licence	B/W £7 Colour £12

YOU WERE BORN

POPULAR MUSIC

Record of the year was 'Tiger Feet' by Mud, released in January which stayed in the charts for nine weeks, four of those at No 1. The Wombles were the most successful 'music act' of 1974 in the UK, with chart albums for more weeks than any other act.

FEBRUARY The Wombles were in the Top 10 for 5 weeks with 'The Wombling Song'. They were a novelty group with musicians dressed as the characters from the children's TV show of the same name.

MARCH 'Seven Seas of Rhye' was the third single released by Queen and their first hit. Written by Freddie Mercury, it motivated him to join the band full-time.

Prawn Cocktail Skips, made by KP Snacks, were similar to Chinese prawn crackers, although smaller and with a finer texture that made them fizz and melt on the tongue. There was a joke, or a tongue-twister, printed on the back of each packet which made them appealing to children.

APRIL Abba won the Eurovision contest for Sweden with their first major single 'Waterloo' which became a worldwide hit.

JUNE French singer Charles Aznavour wrote She as the soundtrack for the British TV series, 'Seven Faces of Woman'.

JULY George McCrae released his debut single 'Rock Your Baby 'which was an early disco hit. It is one of only 40 records to have sold over 10 million physical copies.

AUGUST The Three Degrees had the fourth best-selling track of the year with 'When Will I See You Again,' which topped the chart for two weeks.

SEPTEMBER John Denver had his only major hit single in the UK with 'Annie's Song' which reached No1.

OCTOBER 'Gonna Make You a Star' was the first hit for David Essex, staying for three weeks at the top of the charts.

DECEMBER 'Lucy in The Sky With Diamonds' was an Elton John cover of The Beatles hit song, featuring backing vocals and guitar by John Lennon.

The Christmas No1 was secured by Mud with 'Lonely This Christmas', which sold over 750,000 copies.

1979 The Year

The 1979 Education Act opened the way for progressive trends in schools in reading, writing and number, however, the reality was one of chaos and muddled planning, with some schools reverting to more traditional ways. There were greater cuts in education spending resulting in fewer teachers and larger classes, and increased teachers' strikes. An emphasis on 'topic' rather than 'subject' based teaching arrived with school terms planned around themes, such as the seasons or holidays.

More schools were in favour of a corporate colour scheme of casual clothes rather than a uniform and an increasing number of children took packed lunches to school as individual portion packs of snacks like crisps, Dairylea cheese portions, chocolate and drinks became available in supermarkets. School dinners moved away from the traditional to increasingly feature tempting foods such as chips, fish fingers and pizza.

How Much Did It Cost?

The Average Pay	£5,250 (101 pw)
The Average House	£19,925
Loaf of White Bread	26p
Pint of Milk	14-15p
Pint of Beer	34p
Gallon of Petrol	98p
Newspapers	8p - 15p
To Post a letter in UK	10p
12mnths Road Tax	£50
TV Licence B/W (pre Nov) £12 (10) Colour £34 (25)	

Children At Five

Five in 1979, everything from snacks to toys was available in growing variety. Supermarkets and superstores stocked everything to tempt our children who were now an influence on spending. They were just as likely to eat savoury snacks like Monster Munch as they were sweets or lollies, such as Funny Feet, a moulded strawberry ice cream foot on a stick.

Many toys and games were derived from popular TV programmes and shelves filled with Dr. Who's Tardis, or 'The General' car from Dukes of Hazzard County. In the world of soft toys and dolls, America was a major influence, with Barbie, and Holly Hobbie dolls and their accessories very popular.

YOU WERE FIVE

MUSIC

Art Garfunkel had the best-selling single of 1979 with **Bright Eyes** from the soundtrack of the film 'Watership Down'. It stayed at No1 for six weeks and another soundtrack from a film **Cavatina,** The Deer Hunter by The Shadows reached No9.

Heart of Glass and **Sunday Girl** both became No1s for Blondie whilst **Dreaming** made No2, all three included in the year's top 10 best-sellers.

TV was the family's main entertainment. British favourites 'Are You Being Served' and 'Last of the Summer Wine' were joined by glamorous American imports, 'Dallas' and 'Charlie's Angels'. Programming was geared towards age/gender groups; with children's TV at lunch and teatime, women's 'magazine' programmes like Pebble Mill at One, and sport largely confined to Saturdays.

JANUARY The crowd-pleasing **YMCA** by The Village People was the first new No 1 of the year.

FEBRUARY Frequently recalled as a symbol of female empowerment; **I Will Survive** reached the top for Gloria Gaynor.

MAY **Dance Away** by the rock band Roxy Music was written by Bryan Ferry and although only managing second place in the charts, it became the ninth biggest selling single in the UK this year and one of their best-known songs.

AUGUST Cliff Richard had his first No1 in eleven years with **We Don't Talk Anymore** which stayed four weeks at the top and was the third best-selling single of the year.

OCTOBER **When You're In Love with a Beautiful Woman** by Dr Hook was No1. The song first appeared on the band's 1978 album **Pleasure and Pain**.

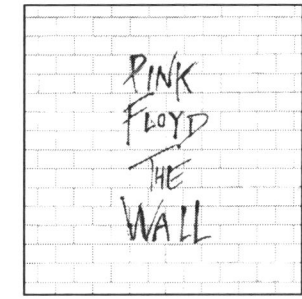

DECEMBER **The Wall**, Pink Floyd's rock opera was released featuring all three parts of **Another Brick in the Wall. Part 2**, written as a protest against rigid schooling.

1985 THE YEAR

1985 was a year with many tragedies. 55 people were killed in the Manchester Air Disaster; 56 people died in the Bradford City FC fire and 39 died in the Heysel Stadium Disaster.

There was football hooliganism, Brixton riots and scientists found the ozone hole. But the devastating Miners' Strike ends after one year; Live Aid pop concerts raise over £50m for famine relief in Ethiopia; the first mobile phone calls in the UK are made; the first UK heart and lung transplant is carried out and the Sinclair C5 has a seven-month life!

The Sinclair C5

British holidaymakers were becoming more adventurous in their choice of holiday destinations with tour operator Instasun offering trips to Florida from only £139 for a week. Cosmos began to offer package tours to China, and Kuoni's best sellers included trips to Thailand and the Maldives.

Closer to home, people started to travel behind the Iron Curtain. Yugotours, which offered trips to Yugoslavia grew to be one of top 10 package holiday operators and UK holidaymakers started to enjoy beach holidays in Bulgaria and Romania.

1985 was a record year for the car industry, with 1.8 million new cars sold in Britain. The new Japanese Nissan factory building in Sunderland, was started in April and completed by Christmas.

Spanish company SEAT began exporting their small, family cars into Britain and production of the first UK built foreign car - the Peugeot 309 began in Coventry.

The Peugeot 309

Eleven In 1985

Eleven-year-olds in 1985 went from being the 'old hands' at primary school to the 'newbies' at their secondary school. Traditional lessons and discipline had given way to more progressive methods in most schools. Much screen advertising was aimed at youngsters who influenced their parent's spending and 'must have' toys this year included Teddy Ruxpin, an animatronic bear with built in cassette player, and Cabbage Patch Dolls, which one had to pay to 'adopt' rather than buy them, and each one came complete with adoption papers.

How Much Did It Cost?

The Average Pay	£11,544 (£222 pw)
The Average House	£43,000
Loaf of White Bread	40p
Pint of Milk	23p
Pint of Beer	77p
Gallon of Petrol	£1.99
Newspapers	18p-23p
To Post a letter in UK	17p
12mnths Road Tax	£100
TV Licence	B/W £18 Colour £58

You Were Eleven

The Dire Straits album **Brothers in Arms** was released and becomes the first compact disc to sell over 1,000,000 copies.

Jennifer Rush had the bestselling single of the year with **The Power of Love** and Madonna had a total of eight top ten hits. **Into the Groove** was her first UK No 1. Foreigner was the first No 1 of the year with **I Want to Know What Love Is**.

JANUARY I Know Him So Well by Elaine Paige and Barbara Dickson was No 1 for four weeks into February and became the second bestselling single of the year..

FEBRUARY Bruce Springsteen added 'uptempo' synthesizer riffs to his sound for the first time in **Dancing in the Dark**. From his album **Born in the USA**, it reached No 4 in the UK but became his biggest hit worldwide.

APRIL We Are the World, the charity single by USA for Africa, stayed at No 1 for two weeks. Written by Michael Jackson and Lionel Richie, it sold in excess of 20m copies.

JUNE A special recording of **You'll Never Walk Alone** was made after the Bradford City FC fire. Performed by The Crowd featuring Gerry Marsden, Paul McCartney and others.

SEPTEMBER Midge Ure, co-writer of the charity single **Do They Know it's Christmas** has his only No 1 as a solo artist with **If I Was**.

DECEMBER The Pet Shop Boys released their **West End Girls**, inspired by TS Eliot's poem, 'The Waste Land', but it did not peak at No 1 until the new year.

Ford Escort

Over 157,000 Ford Escorts found homes in the UK in 1985, making it the best seller ahead of the Vauxhall Cavalier. The saloon version, named the Orion, sold another 65,000 units.

The Vauxhall Cavalier

1990 THE YEAR

In 1990, the Government introduced the Poll Tax, Margaret Thatcher resigned, but Tories stayed in power. Unemployment went up, as did prices, and it was official that we were in a recession.

Nature's wild cards gave us an earthquake in Shropshire, a record temperature of 37.1 degrees in Cheltenham, and a snowstorm in December that paralysed the country for days.

At the beginning of December, the French and English officially shook hands 40 metres below the English Channel, as the Channel Tunnel met up in the middle. Two years after construction first started, a land connection between the two countries was finally made for the first time in 8,000 years.

On the plus side this year new chain stores Aldi, Poundland and Netto opened up; Hampton Court held its 1st Flower Show and Radio 5 was launched by the BBC. On the TV we laughed at the antics of 'Mr. Bean' and the snobbery of Hyacinth Bucket in 'Keeping Up Appearances'.

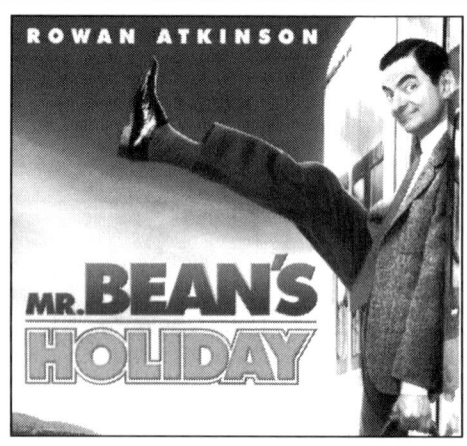

LIFE AT SIXTEEN

Sixteen in 1990, you could fight for your country, or work full-time without your parents' consent and get a National Insurance Number from the Government, but you couldn't buy alcohol in a pub. You could get a licence to drive a scooter or low-powered motorcycle but not a car. You could open a bank account but weren't allowed a credit card. Denim was still universally popular teamed with branded leather trainers whilst the popularity of Bollywood films made ethnic, beaded and animal print fabrics fashionable.

HOW MUCH DID IT COST?

The Average Pay	£12,353 (£238 pw)
The Average House	£58,000
Loaf of White Bread	50p
Pint of Milk	25p
Pint of Beer	1.40p
Gallon of Petrol	£2.13
Newspapers	20p-30p
To Post a letter in UK	22p
12mnths Road Tax	£100
TV Licence	B/W £24 Colour £71

You Were 16

Popular Music

Elton John's **Sacrifice** only achieved poor sales when it was originally released in 1989, but re-released in 1990 as a double A-side with **Healing Hands**, it stayed at No1 for 5 weeks, becoming his first solo single in the UK. **Unchained Melody** by the Righteous Brothers was the top selling single of the year. Originally released in 1965, it featured in the box office hit film 'Ghost' this year, and spent 9 weeks in the charts, 4 of them at No1. Madonna had 4 singles in the Top Ten this year, including her No 1 success **Vogue**.

JANUARY Sinead O'Connor's record **Nothing Compares 2 U** was the second best-selling single of the year. Written originally by Prince, her version was No 1 for 4 weeks.

MARCH German Euro-dance group Snap! released their debut single **The Power** which went to No 1 and became a big club dance favourite.

MAY Best-selling Australian female artist Kylie Minogue, now known as 'The Princess of Pop' released **Better The Devil You Know** which reached No 2.

JUNE Luciano Pavarotti's recording of **Nessun Dorma** brought classical opera to the charts when it was used by the BBC for its coverage of the FIFA World Cup in Italy

NOVEMBER **Ice Ice Baby** was rapper Vanilla Ice's 1st single which became a worldwide hit and brought hip-hop to mainstream audiences.

DECEMBER The Christmas No 1 was **Saviour's Day** by Cliff Richard, the third-top-selling artist in UK singles chart history.

Completely revamped in 1989, the 3rd generation Ford Fiesta became Britain's best-selling car, with 151,475 models sold in 1990, knocking its big brother – the Escort – into second place and the Vauxhall Astra third.

Ford Fiesta

The Vauxhall Astra

13

1995 THE YEAR

1995 was a year with many positives in industry and culture. Sizewell B finally synchronised with the National Grid to bring more affordable and efficient energy. South Korean car manufacturer Daewoo announced plans to build a factory in the UK creating new jobs, and the MG Sports car brand was revived for the first time since 1980. Lancashire Constabulary appointed its first woman Chief Constable, the Pensions Act phased in parity between men's and women's pensions, and pubs could stay open all Sunday afternoons.

Sizewell B Nuclear Power Station

Grunge Fashion

Grunge was an anti-fashion trend, with oversized charity shop clothes that hid the figure, ripped jeans, Doc Marten boots and checked flannel shirts. Magazines like Vogue or Harpers, known for their style and chic featured models dressed in flimsy, floaty ripped dresses worn with biker boots and shapeless cardigans.

Although unemployment was at its lowest for 4 years, we said goodbye to Rumbelows, the electrical retailer, with a loss of over 3,000 jobs, and Barings Bank collapsed from losses by the rogue trader, Nick Leeson. Things became chillier as the Queen urged Charles and Diana to get a divorce '*as soon as possible*' and in December, Britain's lowest temperature of -27.2°C was recorded in the Scottish Highlands.

MOBILE PHONES GO FUCHSIA

Gone were the days of the 'mobile-brick', which Michael Douglas wielded so forcefully in the movie "Wall Street". The new Motorola Flare was launched in the UK by One2One being sold from September 1995 for £129.99. It came in a variety of colours, but not all were to everyone's taste. Writing in the Independent in 1995, film producer Jill Robertson, said that using the fuchsia and black version in Soho was a fashion crime!

HOW MUCH DID IT COST?

The Average Pay	£14,976 (£288 pw)
The Average House	£56,000
Loaf of White Bread	53p
Pint of Milk	36p
Pint of Beer	£1.45
Gallon of Petrol	£2.73
Newspapers	30p-40p
To Post a letter in UK	25p
12mnths Road Tax	£140
TV Licence	B/W £28.50 Colour £86.50

14

You Were 21

Popular Music

Manchester band Oasis became a hot topic in the tabloids with their wild lifestyle, and chart-topping success. **(What's The Story) Morning Glory** became the biggest UK selling album in the 90's.

Acting duo, Robson and Jerome, from the drama series 'Soldier, Soldier' released **Unchained Melody/ White Cliffs of Dover**. It became the best-selling single of 1995 staying at No 1 for 7 weeks, with sales pushing it to platinum status, and went on to become the best-selling single of the decade.

JANUARY Nicki French made a dance cover version of Bonnie Tylers 80's hit **Total Eclipse of The Heart** for the UK 1995 entry in the Eurovision Song Contest.

FEBRUARY Riverdance was an instrumental interval act first performed live at the 1994 Eurovision Song Contest. The record stayed in the Top 10 for 2 weeks.

APRIL Back For Good was Take That's 6th No1 hit, which they debuted at the year's Brit Awards.

AUGUST London band Blur released **Country House** which reached No1 on the same day as their rivals Oasis released their single **Roll With It** which only reached No2. The press dubbed it 'The Battle of Brit Pop'.

NOVEMBER Eccentric Icelandic singer/songwriter Bjork stayed at No4 for 8 weeks with her English version of a 1948 German song **It's Oh So Quiet**. In Britain it became a gold disc, selling more than 400,000 copies.

DECEMBER 25 years after the band broke up, and 15 years after John Lennon's murder, the remaining members of The Beatles released a studio version of **Free As a Bird**, which reached No2 in the charts.

The Playstation games console was aggressively marketed as the best model for young adults, with its low retail price and popular franchises including Gran Turismo, Crash Bandicoot, Tomb Raider and Resident Evil.

15

1974

SPORTING HEADLINES

MARCH The **1974 Grand National** which took place at Aintree Racecourse, Liverpool, was won for the second time by Red Rum ridden by Brian Fletcher. Living up to his name, L'Escargot ridden by Tommy Carberry, came second.

The **Five Nations Championship** was won by Ireland in the forty-fifth series of the Rugby Union championship. It was the team's eighth outright title. Ten matches were played between 19 January and 16 March, and the tournament was closely contested with three of the matches ending in draws.

MAY The **FA Cup Final** between Liverpool and Newcastle United took place at Wembley Stadium. The final, televised live, was watched by a crowd of 100,000 and Liverpool won a one-sided match 3–0 with goals by Kevin Keegan and Steve Heighway. After the third goal, the match commentator said that Newcastle's defence had been "stripped naked" by Liverpool.

JUNE In the 'Love Double' at Wimbledon, American Chris Evert won the Ladies Singles Title for the first time, beating Olga Morozova of the Soviet Union, whilst her fiancé, American Jimmy Connors, beat the Australian Ken Rosewall.

JULY The **1974 Open Championship** was the 103rd Open Championship, held from 10–13 July at Royal Lytham & St Annes Golf Club in Lancashire and was won by Gary Player. He was four strokes ahead of runner-up Peter Oosterhuis. He had also won the US Masters in April.

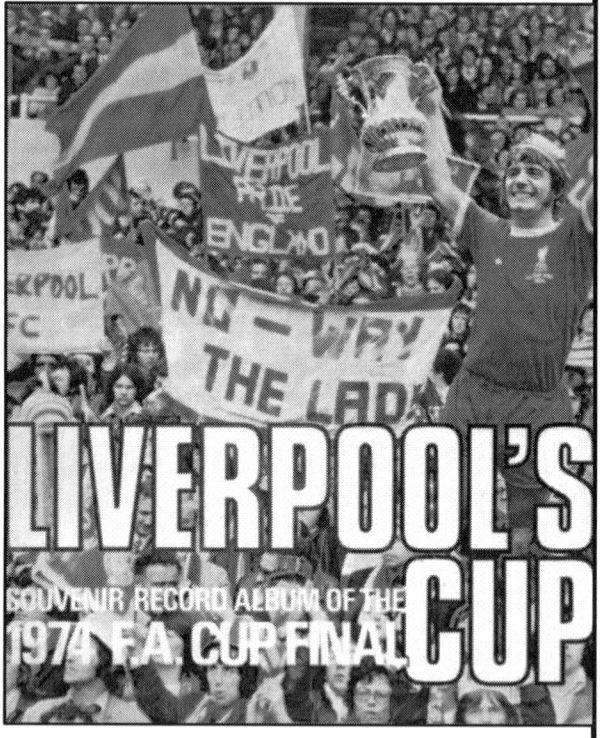

West Germany had been chosen as the host nation for the **FIFA World Cup** back in July 1966. This year they won the title, beating Netherlands 2–1 in the final at the Olympiastadion in Munich. This was their second victory, they also won in 1954.

Eddy Merckx won the **Tour de France**, which made its first visit to the United Kingdom, with a circuit stage on the Plympton By-pass, near Plymouth.

OCTOBER At what was billed as 'The Rumble in The Jungle' held in Zaire, Muhammad Ali regained the **World Heavyweight** boxing title by knocking out George Forman in the eighth round. Ali was voted as Sportsman of the Year by a panel of sports editors from across the United States, for Sports Illustrated Magazine.

Sporting Events

The Ten Cents Beer Baseball Night

This was a promotion hosted by Cleveland Indians during a game against the Texas Rangers at Cleveland Stadium in June 1974, which was meant to improve attendance at the game by offering cups of low alcohol beer for just 10 cents each, a substantial discount on the regular price of 65 cents, with a limit of six beers per purchase but with no limit on the number of purchases made during the game.

Six days earlier during the teams' last meeting, the Indians and the Rangers had been involved in a widely-publicised bench-clearing brawl at Arlington Stadium, where both teams left their dugouts, bullpens, or benches, and charged onto the playing area in order to fight one another. This had angered many Indians fans, who then harboured a grudge against the Rangers, and the game therefore attracted a rowdy and aggressive crowd.

As the game proceeded, on-field incidents and massive alcohol consumption further agitated the audience, many of whom threw lit fireworks or streaked across the playing field, while others sat back smoking marijuana. Most of the sober fans left early, leaving an increasingly drunk and unruly mob behind. A riot erupted in the ninth inning when Wilcox fielded the ball and tagged Randle out, Randle hit him with his forearm. Indians' first baseman Ellis responded by punching Randle, and both benches emptied for a brawl. Fans rushed the field forcing the players to protect themselves with bats, while retreating from the field. After the brawl was broken up, as Indians players and coaches returned to the dugout, they were struck by food and beer hurled by Rangers fans, and the catcher had to be restrained from entering the stands to fight the fans. The chief umpire declared the game to be forfeited in Texas Rangers' favour 3–0 due to the mob's uncontrollable behaviour.

1974

THE TOWERING INFERNO

This American disaster movie had a stellar cast led by Paul Newman and Steve McQueen with Faye Dunaway, Robert Wagner, and Richard Chamberlain alongside the legendary 75-year-old Fred Astaire. As its title suggests, this film is packed with suspense and expensive stunts in a scenario in which anything and everything fails, explodes, or hangs by a thread at great height.

Steve McQueen insisted on doing his stunts himself, and during filming an actual fire broke out on one of the sets and he found himself briefly helping real firefighters put it out.

Although the film cost $14 million to make, the $203.3 million box office, made it the highest grossing film of the year. It was nominated for eight Academy Awards, and won Best Picture, Best Cinematography and Best Editing.

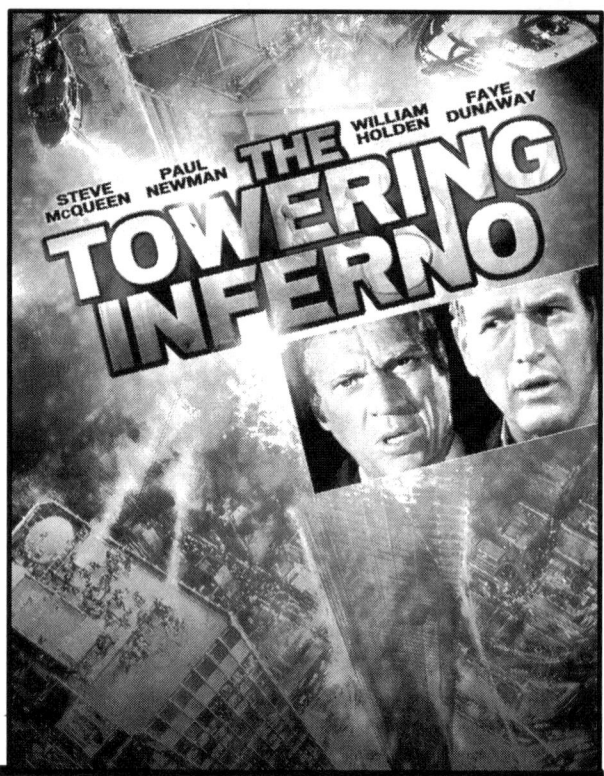

WISH YOU WERE HERE

Aimed at dispelling the January blues, a new travel programme was introduced on television with Judith Chalmers presenting **Wish You Were Here**. It was a series of 30-minute shows about travel and holidays, and was broadcast at peak viewing time, when families would have finished dinner and settled down for an evening's viewing.

The team also included John Carter, Mary Nightingale and former Blue Peter presenter Anthea Turner, but most people will remember seeing calm, unflappable Judith, strolling around beautiful cities, exotic beaches and enjoying luxurious hotels.

As well as destinations, there were helpful hints on foreign exchange, tips on packing, and of course duty free. Although *'all holiday programmes faced the criticism that many of the places visited were beyond the means of many viewers, there were features on holidays closer to home that many found genuinely helpful.'*

CULTURAL EVENTS

POIROT

A new short story collection written by Agatha Christie, entitled **Poirot's Early Cases** was published in September by Collins Crime Club, costing only £2.25.

The collection recounts some of the cases from his early career before he became well known as a detective. Hercule Poirot, the small and dapper Belgian detective was one of Christie's most famous and long-running characters. With incredible powers of observation, serene Gallic charm, and gentle moustache twirling he encourages all Christie's readers to pit their wits against his and see if they too can solve the crime.

The author was made a Dame of the Empire in 1971 for her contributions to literature and entered the Guinness World Records as the best-selling fiction writer of all time, her novels having sold more than two billion copies.

ABBA

In February a little-known quartet of singers from Sweden took the world by storm when they won the Eurovision Song Contest and started a cult sensation in the pop world. Bjorn, Benny, Anetha and Anni-Frid (Frida) first joined forces in 1972 under the name of Festfolk.

Invited by Swedish television to write a song for the National Song Festival the following year, they wrote 'Waterloo' which was chosen as Sweden's entry for Eurovision.

It was at this point they chose the name of **ABBA** for the group, being an acronym made up of the first initials of their names. Singing their upbeat composition in English this time gave them an edge over many other competitors and secured an international future for the group as one of the most followed and best-selling music acts in the history of popular music.

1974

The 'Heimlich Maneuvre'

Henry Heimlich, an American thoracic surgeon discovered a procedure which became known as the 'Heimlich Maneuvre,' which is a technique of using abdominal thrusts to rescue someone who is choking.

Heimlich first published his conclusions in a medical journal in June of that year, and the Chicago Daily News subsequently ran an article about Dr. Heimlich's findings. Later that month, retired restaurant owner Isaac Piha, who had read the article, used the procedure to rescue a choking victim in Washington.

Medical experts have advised that a rescuer should encourage the patient first to expel the obstruction by coughing. As a second measure, the rescuer should deliver five slaps to the back after bending the patient forward.

Abdominal thrusts are recommended only if these methods fail.

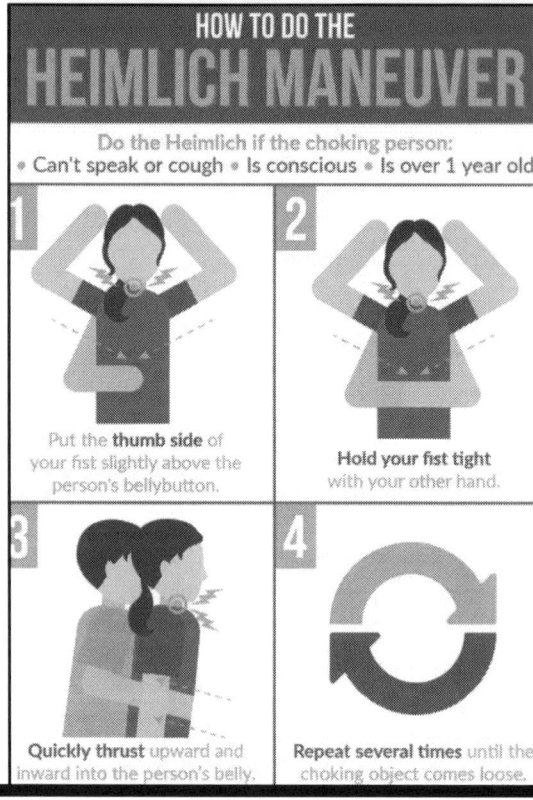

"Lucy"

'Lucy' was the name given to a 3 million year old skeleton of Homo Australopithecus, discovered in November near the Awash River in Ethiopia by Donald Johansen, a paleoanthropologist from Cleveland.

According to his account, he and a colleague spent some time one morning surveying the dusty terrain. On a hunch, he decided to look in a gully that had been previously inspected and found fragments of bone. Over the next three weeks his team found several hundred pieces or fragments of bone, from a single female skeleton.

Following the initial discovery the team celebrated at the camp, and at some point during the evening they named fossil AL 288-1 "Lucy", after the Beatles' song 'Lucy In The Sky With Diamonds' which was being played loudly and repeatedly on a tape recorder in the camp.

SCIENCE AND NATURE

RUBIK'S CUBE

The 3D combination puzzle was invented by Ernő Rubik who worked at the Academy of Applied Arts and Crafts in Budapest. While a professor of design at the academy, he pursued his hobby of building geometric models, one of which was a prototype of the cube, made of 27 wooden blocks.

He was trying to solve the structural problem of moving the parts independently without the entire mechanism falling apart and didn't realise that he had created a puzzle until the first time he scrambled his new Cube and then tried to restore it.

While Rubik became famous for inventing this 'Magic Cube' and other puzzles, much of his current work involves the promotion of science in education with the aim to engage students in science, mathematics, and problem solving at a young age.

CHINESE EARTHQUAKE

A violent earthquake occurred in Yunnan Province in Southern China, in May at 3am., when townspeople were asleep. The earthquake consisted of several shocks of magnitudes below 5, over 2-3 seconds. These were followed by several shocks of magnitude 7 over a period of a minute affecting an area of over 400,000 sq.km. Triggering many landslides around the epicentre in Zhaotong, the greatest damage was caused by rock avalanches, with 28,000 houses destroyed and a further 38,000 damaged. However, houses with wooden frames seem to have remained relatively undamaged. The number of deaths varied but reports say that up to 20,000 people may have died with a further 1,600 injured. The largest landslide formed a dam up to 30 metres (98ft) high across the Yangtze River turning the valley above it into a lake.

1974 LIFESTYLES OF

NORTHERN SOUL

A movement emerged in Northern England and The Midlands in the early 1970s, based on a particular style of Black American Soul Music with a heavy beat and fast tempo. Recordings most prized by enthusiasts were by lesser-known artists, released in limited numbers on relatively obscure labels, rather than the more popular Motown successes.

By 1974, coach loads of devotees would descend on Saturday evenings at venues such as The Wigan Casino or The Twisted Wheel in Manchester to dance in all-nighters until 8am on Sunday morning, when the coaches would drive them home.

As the favoured beat became more 'uptempo', Northern Soul dancing became more athletic featuring spins, karate kicks and backdrops made easier by the baggy trousers or flowing skirts and flat shoes worn by the dancers.

IN VOGUE

Ladies' fashions in the mid 1970's owed a great deal to the Hippie styles which were made popular at the end of the 60's after the Woodstock Festival in New York State. Fabrics were printed in strong colours, featuring Indian designs, and embellished with fringing, beads or folk embroidery. Bell-bottoms, frayed jeans, midi skirts, and ankle-length maxi dresses were worn with platform shoes known as 'dolly mixtures' which resembled children's summer sandals.

Boots were also at the height of their popularity, the most popular being 'Go-Go Boots' with a shiny wet look that was wrinkled. By 1974 T-shirts were boldly printed with slogans, sports teams, and other designs. All styles of hat were trendy, with floppy hats the most versatile, looking good with both simple jeans and a peasant blouse to your best mini dress.

EVERYDAY PEOPLE

HEALTHY EATING

The rise of the back-to-the-landers, who became the backbone of the organic movement, had their origins in Hippie culture, which rebelled against the established order of industrialised everything. They helped to set up farmers' markets in order to sell directly to customers.

They made connections with restaurants such as Alice Water's 'Chez Panisse' in California, who embraced the 'farm to table' ideal. This was the start of the slow-food revolution which re-introduced us to the ethnic foods that the West, in its progress, thought it had left behind, such as lentils, brown rice, organic produce and yogurt.

The cuisine that was counter cultural in the late 1960s, started to become mainstream in the 1970s, opening the way for the flavours from Eastern European, Asian, and Latin American cuisines that would become so popular later in the decade.

HOME HELPERS

The reality in 1974 was that most women had to work to make ends meet as prices rose and wages stagnated. Labour saving gadgets now came into their own. There were trips to the Bejam Freezer Supermarket to fill the now affordable chest freezer stored in the garage. The Hostess Trolley became a status symbol for lower-middle-class housewives who entertained, creating the illusion that no effort had been involved in preparing a candlelit supper.

The Monday morning alarm could be softened with a freshly brewed cuppa, courtesy of a Goblin Teasmade which sat on the bedside table. And for the winter evenings there was the electric slow-cooker that used no more energy than a light bulb to cook your meal, while you slaved all day over a hot typewriter in the office.

January 1st - 7th 1974

IN THE NEWS

Tuesday 1 — **"Traffic Jams and Record Crowds"** Over 10,000 people turned out to see Prince Charles and Lady Jane Wellesley at Sandringham. Mindful of the Government's call to save petrol, the Royal Family travelled to Church by minibus.

Wednesday 2 — **"3-Day Week Introduced"** Due to a 4,000-gallon oil delivery delay, a major London hospital, Brook General, cannot accept new patients, or emergencies.

Thursday 3 — **"Whitehouse Call on Councils"** Mary Whitehouse proposed that broadcasting advisory councils should be made up of at least 50% women to warn against the current level of vulgar language and sexual innuendo on TV.

Friday 4 — **"Buckingham Palace Announcement"** Princess Anne's husband, Captain Mark Phillips, has been appointed as personal Aide-de-Camp to the Queen. It is a personal honour which the Sovereign confers on serving officers in the Royal Family. There are no specific duties attached to this post.

Saturday 5 — **"Bus Agreement May Mean Women Drivers"** London Transport has agreed to allow women to drive London buses, despite cab seats which are designed for drivers taller than 5ft 8in and pedals on older buses which may be too heavy for women.

Sunday 6 — **"Museum Entry"** Museums are to start charging entrance fees of 10p for adults and 5p for children, except in July and August, when it will be increased to 20p. The government argue that people are willing to pay for the pleasure of visiting museums and galleries.

Monday 7 — **"Cost of Living"** A recent survey of 63 British towns shows that living in the South East is more expensive, but that average wages are rising faster in the Midlands and Scotland. East Anglia is the cheapest area to live in.

HERE IN BRITAIN

"Expensive Passion"

The Earl's Court Boat Show this year features a Bahamian setting, with boats floating in a reproduction of Nassau harbour. There are more foreign boats on show than previous years, possibly because of the superior design and styling of the foreign exhibits.

French yachts dominate the smaller classes while among the power boats at Earls Court, some of the most striking come from America. The epitome of glamour however must be the 42' motor cruiser from Italy which at 73,000 Euros is the most expensive craft on view..

AROUND THE WORLD

"Changing Shape of Fashion"

The exhibition "Inventive Clothes 1909-1939" organized by the former Editor of Vogue in America, has opened at the Metropolitan Museum of Art in New York, featuring designs by Chanel, Schiaparelli and Vionnet.

The silhouette has dramatically changed so the display mannequins had to be altered, '*as vulgar forms with prominent "bazooms" would never do*' so '*up came the museum's carpenters, and the "bazooms were sawn off*'. The evening opened with a dinner at $150 a head after which the guests were able to wander round the exhibition.

WE WILL ESCAPE

ESCAPE MUSEUM COLDITZ CASTLE

An exhibition of items of escape equipment and other curios from the WWII German prison, Colditz Castle, has opened at the Imperial War Museum and more than 300 'old boys' from Colditz assembled for the opening event. The collection of forged work passes, saws made out of chipped razors, and maps concealed in the fabric of playing cards along with photographs and models of the prison are a therapeutic antidote to the fiction of the good, clean, sentimental fun that is depicted in the popular television series.

Among the previous prison inmates attending were RAF fighter pilot, Douglas Bader, Mr Airey Neave, MP, and Dr Reinhold Eggers, the German camp security officer. The displays include items which were only discovered when the Radio Times took four former prisoners on a sentimental journey back to Colditz - which is now a mental hospital 20 miles south-east of Leipzig in the Democratic Republic of East Germany. There they rediscovered the secret radio shack high under the eaves of the castle roof and still untouched since the war ended. The hatch contained makeshift equipment which was vitally important 30 years ago, an escape rope made from bed sheets, a forged master key that would open most of the doors in the castle, emergency escape kits and a civilian raincoat which had been "*liberated*" from an unsuspecting German visitor to the castle.

Also displayed are numerous items of memorabilia which have been lent from private collections, including a hand carved chess set, the black pieces being caricatures of the German officers. There is also a replica of the glider made of wood and bed sheets, which they planned to launch off the castle roof.

January 8th – 14th 1974

IN THE NEWS

Tuesday 8 — **"Milk Bottle Shortage"** As customers fail to return empties, the shortage has worsened as glass makers cannot supply the extra 600 million bottles needed this year.

Wednesday 9 — **"The Queen to Visit the Wellesleys"** The Queen and Prince Phillip will visit the Duke of Wellington's country estate for the game fair. Lady Jane Wellesley, a close friend of Prince Charles, was a guest at Sandringham over the New Year holiday.

Thursday 10 — **"Help for Africans"** A number of bursaries have been funded by a British pharmaceutical firm to allow Africans from the Transkei homeland to study medicine in Britain.

Friday 11 — **"Promise to Farmers of Fair Milk Price"** Fears that narrow profit margins on milk will erode confidence among dairy farmers, has resulted in a call for an increase in farm prices. It is hoped that production next winter will not be compromised.

Saturday 12 — **"TVZ Launched in Tanzania"** To commemorate the 10th anniversary of the Zanzibar Revolution, the President inaugurated TVZ. The first colour television station south of the Sahara, it will broadcast in Swahili and English.

Sunday 13 — **"No Government Rules"** The Minister for Population said that although Britain's birth rate is slowing and there is a need to stabilise the population, *"The Government can only point the way. To try to stipulate family size, regardless of the individual's circumstances would be quite wrong. Each family must make up its own mind."*

Monday 14 — **"Keep 50 mph Limit"** Falling accident figures in East Anglia have been attributed to the 50-mph speed limit imposed in the area last year. The Chief Constable of the Mid-Anglia Police Force has urged that it should be retained.

HERE IN BRITAIN

"It's Rocket Science"

Following the scrapping of the Blue Streak project in the Lake District, one of the trials managers for Hawker-Siddley has refused two lucrative aerospace jobs in the South, because he does not wish to leave Cumberland.

He will sign on for unemployment benefit in Carlisle, saying, *"I won't be tripping over any pride on the way to the dole queue. Our family life in Cumberland is priceless. I feel like a 'drop-out', but I am leaving the rat race to others. Cumberland is one of the last outposts of civilisation."*

AROUND THE WORLD

"Howzat!"

An English woman has successfully given birth to 3 boys and 3 girls in a Cape Town hospital. The six babies, born by cesarean section appear to have a good chance of being the first set of sextuplets in the world to successfully survive.

The pregnancy, which followed the use of a hormone fertility drug, lasted 37 weeks aided by a muscle relaxant drug called Orciprinaline, a muscle relaxant which was designed for the treatment of asthma. It calms the involuntary muscles of the body, including those that bring about birth contractions.

Three Day Week

Retailers have been achieving near normal illumination with the aid of battery lamps, storm lanterns, and candles until 2.30 pm, after which they are allowed to use electricity for lighting according to the Government's energy-saving regulations. But there have been grumblings over the ambiguity of the rulings. One sweet shop owner has been keeping the lights on all day as he was classed as a food shop by the Retail Distributors' Association but then told by the Chamber of Commerce that he was not. Small businesses are complaining that the larger stores have unfair trading advantages over them because they usually have their own electricity generators, so can be lit all day. The manager of a furniture store said *"We were told we could use half our normal lighting for half of each day. Instead of doing that, we are using a quarter of the normal lighting for the whole of each day. It all works out to the same."*

All shops are allowed to have lights on over the tills to protect cash takings, and on stairwells for safety reasons. However, some traders are blatantly ignoring all instructions, and using their lighting all day in order to encourage shoppers. This has led to rivals informing on them to the Police and the Electricity Board. Another downside to the restrictions has been the rise in shoplifting, made all the easier in unlit aisles. Next week, shops in the Southeast will be permitted lights only from 9.30am to 12.30pm, giving rise to the complaint that they will have to close at 4.30 in the afternoon or they will lose more in pilfering than they sell. One police officer said, *"We are not clued up on this and I cannot comment."* while Scotland Yard say 'local forces are responsible'.

January 15th - 21st 1974

IN THE NEWS

Tuesday 15 — **"Turning Coal Away"** The Labour MP for Swindon claims that fuel stocks are so high at power stations that deliveries of coal are being turned away. In his opinion the 3-day working week was *"precipitate and unnecessary."*

Wednesday 16 — **"Larger Green Belt"** The total area of the Green Belt around the main cities in England and Wales is to be virtually doubled. It is calculated that eventually this will amount to 3,000 square miles.

Thursday 17 — **"Gaddafi Financing Terrorism"** France's newspaper 'Minute' reports that funds from Libyan oil have been transferred via the Libyan Embassy in Rome to Gaddafi's Al Wicab guerrilla fighters.

Friday 18 — **"Tribal Medicine Plan"** A scheme in Canberra will encourage medical practitioners to work closely with Aboriginal witch doctors, to integrate traditional Stone Age folk medicine with modern practices.

Saturday 19 — **"Lights on for the Toothbrush"** The Minister for Energy, has admitted that he was wrong to ask people to clean their teeth in the dark in order to save electricity - *"The suggestion I made on radio the other day was not a practical one."*

Sunday 20 — **"Centre Point Occupied"** More than 100 demonstrators protesting about the housing shortage, occupied the controversial empty office block in central London. They infiltrated the security organisation which guards it.

Monday 21 — **"Fewer Students"** Colleges are likely to reduce the number of student admissions next autumn as universities are facing a cut of between £20m and £40m in their grant, made to cover staff salaries, running costs of departments, laboratories and libraries.

HERE IN BRITAIN

"The Chippie Girls"

Waitresses from a Hull fish restaurant have taken their case to Court so they can continue to take pride in their work and keep customers happy. For years the restaurant had a reputation for quick service, but after a change in management policy, the number of tables increased, and customers were left waiting for their orders.

Staff complaints to the manager were ignored, so they went on strike - not for money, but their professional pride. The court ruled in their favour, and normal service has been resumed.

AROUND THE WORLD

"Football Chase"

Police fought with hundreds of rioting football supporters who chased a referee, Vittorio Benedetti, across Catanzaro, a town in southern Italy, for three hours, and then tried to break into the house where he took refuge.

They were angry because he had failed to award Catanzaro two penalty kicks in its match against the visiting team from rivals, Palermo, the capital city of Sicily. The game ended in an unsatisfactory, 1-1 draw. At least eight policemen and one Catanzaro supporter were slightly injured, and ten people were arrested.

CAN GOLD & COPPER DIAGNOSE DIABETES?

Diabetes is a medical condition which can be managed successfully if diagnosed early enough, although it may be present in some people before any symptoms have appeared, and delays in diagnosis can lead to complications as the disease progresses. However, one patient has noticed something interesting which is now being followed up by the British Diabetics Association. The wife of a Nobel prize winning chemist noticed that gold started staining her skin black when she wore her jewellery. Some weeks later, following blood tests, she was diagnosed with diabetes, and prescribed insulin. Shortly afterwards she realised that the black marks from her jewellery had disappeared. Suspecting there might be a link between the marks and her illness, she decided to conduct an experiment. She took an overdose of glucose and the marks returned, confirming her suspicions.

Experts at Guy's Hospital say pure gold is too soft to be used on its own for jewellery and is usually blended with copper or silver and that the staining could happen if fatty acids in the skin caused the base metals and gold to part chemically. Once the metals had parted, the gold could be worn away, leaving fine particles on the skin that would look like a black mark. Diabetes is known to cause many variations in the chemical make-up of the body so that a reaction of this kind would be reasonable, although they agreed it is odd that this phenomenon has not been noticed before with such a common disorder. The Diabetics Association have now launched a survey, asking diabetes sufferers whether they have noticed the presence of the tell-tale black marks on their skin underneath gold bracelets or rings. An early warning from the gold reaction could simplify detection of unsuspected diabetes.

January 22ND - 28TH 1974

IN THE NEWS

Tuesday 22 — **"Royal Visit"** Princess Margaret arrived in Nicosia for a three-day visit to Cyprus. She is the first member of the Royal Family to visit since Cyprus became independent in 1960.

Wednesday 23 — **"30 Years Water Supply"** Five new reservoirs and development of the Dee estuary for water storage have been recommended by the Water Resources Board. This will provide England and Wales with an adequate water supply for the next 30 years.

Thursday 24 — **"Cost of Bread and Butter"** The EEC 'butter mountain' has shrunk to four weeks' supply and the National Farmers Union are predicting sharp increases in price of 3p or 4p a pound. At the same time, the large baking groups are proposing an increase in the cost of bread and flour.

Friday 25 — **"Getaway Taxi"** A taxi driver was paid £100 each time he drove a gang of armed robbers to and from banks in the Southeast for them to rob. Now living and owning a large farm in Camborne, Cornwall, he was jailed for nine years.

Saturday 26 — **"Stop South Africa Rugby Tour"** MPs have called for the cancellation of the British Lions Rugby Tour of South Africa, as, *"It will give the impression that we ... are indifferent to the misery and degradation of coloured South Africans."*

Sunday 27 — **"Pedal Power"** Over 1,300 bicycles has been issued to cadets at the Royal Military Academy, Sandhurst, to help save fuel in travelling to and from their training grounds.

Monday 28 — **"Exam Lure"** The Associated Examining Board is to introduce a worthwhile examination to give reluctant fifth form students an incentive to stay on at school for an extra year until they are 17. It will cover contemporary topics such as environmental issues, social and community studies, and government.

HERE IN BRITAIN
"A Fashion Mistake"

A freak snowstorm took some day trippers from Burnley by surprise when it swept across the Lake District fells. Members of the Patterdale Mountain Rescue Team, who were on a training exercise, were amazed to see the party of women and children obviously in difficulties, 1,800ft up a mountainside.

They came across the group, including a child of four, purely by chance. Having set off walking in bright, sunny conditions, the women, some in fashion shoes, seemed dazed by the sudden change in the weather.

AROUND THE WORLD
"Save Britain Appeal"

President Idi Amin has set up a special fund to help Britain overcome its economic crisis and several thousand Ugandan shillings have already been donated together with a personal gift of 50,000 shillings (over £3,000).

He requested a special aircraft to pick up supplies of vegetables and wheat collected by Ugandans in response to his "Save Britain" appeal, saying that Uganda did not have the facilities to send the food and urged the Prime Minister to *"react quickly so as not to discourage the Ugandans from donating more"*.

Films - A Double Take

The identical Boulting twins have now worked in the film industry for over 37 years as directors and producers, yet still show no signs of retiring. Passionately socialist and outspoken they feel that irreverence is one of their major contributions to the industry. *"Our chief source of pride is that we've managed to aggravate, provoke, irritate ... practically every side of the business. I think we're now accepted, rather like the local public lavatory."*

They became obsessed with the idea of film making aged eight when they went to see Rudolf Valentino in the silent movie 'The Four Horsemen of the Apocalypse' four times in a week. During their career they have produced over 30 films, some winning international film awards, and starring British greats such as Richard Attenborough, John le Mesurier, Ian Carmichael, and Terry Thomas. Productions like 'Brighton Rock', 'The Guinea Pig', and 'Lucky Jim', were uniquely British in an increasingly American market. Although success in terms of revenue has been variable, the recent 'Twisted Nerve' and 'There's A Girl in My Soup' have been box office hits. 'I'm All Right Jack', was one of Peter Sellers' greatest performances as shop steward Fred Kite.

Their latest offering 'Soft Beds, Hard Battles' stars Sellers again playing six different characters, including Adolf Hitler, a British assassin and a Gestapo leader. It sets out to reveal how all the critical events of the Second World War were inspired by the activities inside a Parisian brothel. The brothers offer the opinion that it is *"an example of how wars are won not by brilliant leadership but by accident and 'monumental cock-ups'"*. Once described as the youngest, most enterprising and daring of producers in the British film industry, social historians studying changes in post-war Britain will find rich pickings in their work.

JAN 29TH – FEB 4TH 1974

IN THE NEWS

Tuesday 29 — **"Gold Medal for England"** England won their first Commonwealth Gold medal in swimming since 1962. Brian Brinkley won the 200 metres butterfly race in the games in Christchurch, New Zealand.

Wednesday 30 — **"Kosher Diet Refused"** A prisoner who is an Orthodox Jew has been on hunger strike in Parkhurst and force fed by tube for 819 days, because the prison has refused to provide him Kosher food.

Thursday 31 — **"I Won't Give Evidence"** President Richard Nixon has refused to appear as a witness in the trial of his former chief aide John Ehrlichman, a key figure in the Watergate scandal.

Friday Feb 1 — **"Free Teeth Care"** A dental hygiene course is to be carried out in Rome's secondary schools. Each child will be given a free toothbrush and tube of toothpaste.

Saturday 2 — **"Scarlet Pimpernel Arrested"** Ronald Biggs, known to Scotland Yard as the "Scarlet Pimpernel" of the £2.5m train robbery, is behind bars in a prison cell in Brazil. Flying Squad officers who flew to Rio de Janeiro are standing by for instructions.

Sunday 3 — **"Clay Cross Rebels Face Further Fines"** The rebel councillors at Clay Cross, Derbyshire, are to hold an official meeting even though it could cost them £50 each. They were disqualified from holding office by the High Court last year, for refusing to increase council rents.

Monday 4 — **"M62 Coach Bomb"** 12 people were feared dead and over 30 badly wounded when a private coach blew up near Leeds in the early hours. Servicemen and their families were travelling back home to an army camp in Yorkshire.

HERE IN BRITAIN

"Better Than a Rubber Duck!"

A newspaper asked for tips on energy saving, and the prize was won by Mrs Ida Jones, with a slogan about sharing a bath to save gas. However, she has upset two MPs! *"They are a pair of fuddy-duddies"*, she said, *"People have been sharing a bath for years. It's better than having a rubber duck"*.

In the early years of her marriage, Mrs. Jones recounted that she and her husband often shared a bath and not just for economic reasons. *"For young couples I would say it was a recipe for a happy marriage."*

AROUND THE WORLD

"Traffic Police in Court"

Almost half the traffic cops of Florence, or Polizia Stradale as they are called in Italy, were summoned to appear in court this week on charges of abandoning their posts during a strike for higher wages last year.

They felt they had no option but to strike because the police are classed as part of the armed forces, who have no workers' rights. Unfortunately, in Italy a policeman who demonstrates against the Government or Parliament in this way may be court-martialled on sedition charges.

CHURCHILL'S PROSE

This year will be the centenary of Winston Churchill's birth, and to mark the occasion a new edition of all his writings and books is to be published. The sheer volume of his literary output alone will render this a major task, however the former statesman's undeniably cavalier approach to accuracy will make more headaches than usual for the editor in charge. He freely admitted that *'he knew small Latin and less Greek'*, leading to many classical mis-quotes, and his geography was often inaccurate, his maps quite frankly misleading, so the amount of correction will be considerable enough to warrant an additional commentary to be published as an appendix.

However not all the changes are due to inaccuracy or carelessness. Times have changed, and so have names; many modern readers would have had some difficulty with the old-fashioned spellings. What was known as Currachee at the beginning of the century is now Karachi, whilst variations in the spelling of the same name such as Chile and Chili were commonplace then but might cause confusion now. The editor is keen however to explain that "*Clearly we don't alter anything unless it is fairly clear that it is a mistake that he would have wanted corrected.*"

The original number of fifty books will be condensed into thirty-four volumes, each hand bound in calfskin vellum and printed on paper designed to last for 500 years. Volume 1 is imminent, and production will be continuing until November 1975. So far 300 of the run of 3000 copies has been pre-sold, but at £945 for each set, the market, like the edition, is limited, and the editor is about to embark on a promotional tour of North America and Australia to drum up business.

February 5th - 11th 1974

IN THE NEWS

Tuesday 5 — **"Biggs Stays in Rio"** Brazil has prevented train robber Ronald Biggs from being taken back to Britain. The dramatic decision came only hours before Biggs was due to fly from Rio de Janeiro to London with a Scotland Yard escort.

Wednesday 6 — **"Youths Face Jail for Sacrilege"** Six American teenagers were arrested for climbing on a giant statue of Buddha and taking photographs. They have pleaded guilty to charges of sacrilege in a court in Thailand and each face fines and three years' imprisonment.

Thursday 7 — **"BBC Under Fire"** The BBC have been criticised by the main advisory body over broadcasts on industrial disputes. This reflects public disquiet that such broadcasts aren't improving the likelihood of settlements.

Friday 8 — **"General Election Called"** Prime Minister Ted Heath closed parliament and wrote to the National Union of Mineworkers asking them to postpone tomorrow's scheduled miners' strike until after a General Election later this month.

Saturday 9 — **"Special Dispensation"** The Department of Energy has granted exemption from the 3-day week restrictions to firms printing any election material and postal voting rules. This has also been extended to printers still working on the new electoral register.

Sunday 10 — **"Maori Demonstration in New Zealand"** Maori's threw a petrol bomb and fireworks in protest against British sovereignty when the Queen and the Duke of Edinburgh visited Treaty House in Waitangi, North Island, on their tour of New Zealand.

Monday 11 — **"Estate of Greek Kings Becomes a National Park"** The summer residence of the former Greek royal family has been declared a national park by the President.

HERE IN BRITAIN

"A New Modern Image"

A Leicestershire Women's Institute member regrets she hasn't attended meetings recently as they clash with her career. She enjoys flower arranging and supports their conservation campaign, but the 27-year-old has recently taken a job as a stripper. *"To be honest, the money is the big attraction, but as a mother I would not do anything to be ashamed of."*

One member of the committee admitted they weren't aware of her job but said, *"As a W.I. member she will know what's good taste. And we are supposed to be getting a new modern image."*

AROUND THE WORLD

"Dinosaur Eggs"

A clutch of fossilised dinosaur eggs has been unearthed in France. The find, which is now in the Natural History Museum in Aix-en-Provence, was discovered by two young Frenchmen who run a restaurant close to where a pipe line digger unearthed them.

There are 7 eggs in total, several with shells in a good state of preservation. They measure between 12" and 18" across and weigh up to 121b. The museum director says this further proves that the whole Mediterranean coastal region was densely inhabited by prehistoric creatures.

SAVING RURAL WALES

In many parts of rural Wales, house prices are inflated by holiday and second home seekers, a practice which has given rise to the formation of small housing groups which buy up rural homes, refurbish them and then let them relatively cheaply to young Welsh families who might otherwise leave the area. Being small, the housing groups have a grossly unequal struggle, which has led the people of Llanaelhaearn, a small village of 300 inhabitants on the Lleyn Peninsula, to form a Limited Company. The village doctor calls it "a step in our struggle for a future".

Whilst all over Wales communities such as this are decaying, the villagers here refuse to do nothing. Depopulation and unemployment, migration of families in search of opportunity or just a home they can afford to buy or rent, is a common cause of rural anxiety, closely followed by regret at seeing old traditions, national language and ways of life slowly disappearing. This has led groups to take direct action in protest by occupying holiday homes or disrupting auction sales. But whilst this action gains publicity, other villagers would rather take a more positive approach to change, by building up local business or craft industries.

It is this course of action that Llanaelhaearn has taken, with 260 eligible people each buying one share in the company, which will raise money for local industry and act as an agency to attract the right kind of work to the community. The limited liability in turn will protect the shareholders. *"We have a dread of our community ending up like the village of Rhyd, in Merioneth, where only two cottages are not holiday homes. But it is no good complaining about people leaving and doing nothing about it. Jobs are the key."*

February 12th - 18th 1974

IN THE NEWS

Tuesday 12 — **"Record Transfer"** Bob Latchford, of Birmingham City, becomes the most expensive football transfer to date. Everton have paid a record £350,000 for their new striker.

Wednesday 13 — **"Petrol Price Increases"** Pump prices have risen by 5p a gallon to cover the increase in oil prices imposed by the Middle East. Maximum prices will be 51p for five-star petrol, and 50p for four-star petrol. Diesel increases by 8p a gallon.

Thursday 14 — **"More Complaints Over Meals"** British people seem to be more willing to complain about poor food and customer service these days, which can only result in a long overdue improvement in the standard of hospitality.

Friday 15 — **"Unusual Fine"** A driver has been banned for 12 months and ordered to pay costs and a fine of only 40p for drunk driving. The magistrates felt that with losing his job as a delivery driver, it was unnecessary to 'pile on the agony'.

Saturday 16 — **"Wife to See Biggs Again"** Train robber Ronnie Biggs' wife has requested permission to visit her husband in private in his Brazilian jail. It is rumoured they are contemplating divorce, to allow him to marry his Brazilian girlfriend to avoid repatriation to Britain.

Sunday 17 — **"Motorway Speeding Fines"** 29 motorists appeared before a special sitting of magistrates at Newport Pagnell, Buckinghamshire, after being charged with exceeding the 50-mph speed limit on the M1 motorway.

Monday 18 — **"Stowaway Slips Heathrow Security"** A 15-year-old American schoolboy said that apart from one or two questions by an airport official, he had no trouble in entering Britain after stowing away on a jumbo jet at San Francisco.

HERE IN BRITAIN

"First Transmission of Bagpuss"

The TV programme "Bagpuss" was first broadcast this week. The animation featuring a "saggy, old cloth cat" had only 13 episodes, but the programme regularly remained a firm favourite down the years.
Supporting the baggy pink and white cat were various other characters; the mice carved on the side of the "mouse organ", a rag doll made of scraps, called Madeleine, and Gabriel the toad. Professor Yaffle, the carved wooden woodpecker, was based on the dry-humoured philosopher Bertrand Russell, whom Oliver Postgate, the creator, had once met.

AROUND THE WORLD

"New US Tabloid Without Nudity"

A new tabloid newspaper has been introduced into America aiming to bring entertaining and informative news to the people. The format is similar to our own British production, The Sun, but without the nudity, which Rupert Murdoch feels is a step too far for the American public.

He is spending $5m on launching "The National Star" in the United States and hopes to sell three million copies a week by the spring. There are six pages of sport, a big section devoted to competitions and readers' letters and at least half a page of politics.

VALENTINE'S DAY

Originally a Christian celebration on the Feast of St Valentine, this day has become a day for lovers around the world irrespective of religion. According to tradition, Saint Valentine, a young Christian priest in pagan Rome, restored sight to the blind daughter of his jailer, then wrote her a letter signed "Your Valentine" as a farewell before his execution. It was celebrated initially with small tokens of ribbon or a poem to your loved one, but during the 18th century, confectionery, flowers and greetings cards were exchanged, with little reference any more to the Christian origin of the day. By the end of the Victorian era most cards were mass produced rather than handmade, which gradually paved the way for the commercialism which is associated with the celebration we have today. However, some traditions still die hard, and many prefer an old-fashioned approach, favouring red roses, or chocolates over the more modern choice of sexy underwear or "adult toys".

Many countries celebrate in the same way as Britain, but different traditions are found in others. In Italy a key is given as a symbol of the 'key to unlock another's heart'. Finland and Estonia look on it as a day to remember friends rather than significant others, as is the case in China, where the celebration is held on The Day of 7's, or the 7th day of the 7th month in the Lunar calendar. In South Korea, women give chocolate to men on February 14th, then men give white chocolate to women on White Day a month later on March 14th. On the 14th of April, called Black Day, those who did not receive anything on February or March 14th, go to a Chinese-Korean restaurant to eat Jajangmyeon or black noodles and lament their 'single life'.

February 19th – 25th 1974

IN THE NEWS

Tuesday 19   "Popular Seats" Nominations for the candidates for the General Election now total over 2,000 across the major parties in Britain, the nationalists in Scotland and Wales, and the main parties in Northern Ireland.

Wednesday 20   "Woman Rejected" A lady was rejected again in her 2nd attempt to become an alderman of the City of London when the court found that she was not "a fit and proper" person, despite overwhelming public support. A statement announced the decision had nothing to do with her gender.

Thursday 21   "Sotheby's Sale" A silver model of Bishop's Rock Lighthouse including rocks, dated 1858, was sold for £1900 to the Trinity House Corporation which is responsible for over 90 British lighthouses.

Friday 22   "New Threat to Soviet Ballet Star" Former star of the Leningrad Ballet, Valery Panov, has been ordered to leave Russia immediately, without his wife, in order to avoid possible enforced deportation.

Saturday 23   "Pakistan Recognises Bangladesh" Pakistan extended formal diplomatic recognition to Bangladesh, its amputated eastern wing, two years and two months after losing a bitter war with India that led to Bangladesh's emergence as an independent country.

Sunday 24   "£50 Bill For Navy's Incontinent Bomb Sniffer" A sniffer dog which accompanied an inspection party aboard a Scottish boat unfortunately fouled the crews' bunks. The Admiralty have been asked to pay £50 in compensation.

Monday 25   "A Doctors' Worth' Complaining they are underpaid, French doctors say that they earn less than tradesmen. Surgeons say they are paid 280 francs for taking out a man's appendix whereas upholsterers can earn 630 francs for recovering a sofa.

HERE IN BRITAIN

"Bossy Boots Reigns"

Charles Cruft was the general manager of a dog biscuit manufacturer, and the founder of the famous dog show which was named after him in 1886. It was sold in 1942, following the death of its founder, to The Kennel Club, who established the rules of the competition. This year's Supreme Champion, a St Bernard named "Burtonswood Bossy Boots" was challenged as ineligible by another owner, as they said, 'a judge at Cruft's had handled the dog at another show within the past year', but this claim was proved to be false, and the title stands.

AROUND THE WORLD

"Up, Up and Away"

A Colonel in the US Army was suspended from nine transparent balloons somewhere over the ocean, attempting to be the first man to fly a balloon across the Atlantic. The 48yr old reserve officer, lifted off from an airport in Harrisburg, Pennsylvania, with the gondola attached to 10 large helium filled balloons. On his way to the coast however, one balloon burst, keeping him a bit below his scheduled 39,000ft altitude. According to information on the jet streams he is hoping to ride, he should be over Spain in three or four days.

Costly Doll's Houses

Christie's often auction antique dolls' houses, but this week a record price of £630 was paid for an American example, dated 1870, in the vernacular style of a clapboard villa with pinnacle gables. Traditionally they were commissioned pieces made to order by craftsmen, not for children, but wealthy adults, as a mark of their social class. Known as 'baby houses' in the 17th century, from the English word meaning doll, the interiors displayed the height of fashion in design and furnishings and were trophy collections owned by the few merchants and their wives living in the cities of Holland, England and Germany who had enough wealth to afford them.

As time progressed, they became less of a status symbol and more akin to the models we are familiar with today. Used in the 18th century as a means of training wealthy teenage girls in household management, by the 19th century they had become an elaborate toy consigned to the nursery. In 1904 Beatrix Potter based her book 'The Tale of Two Bad Mice' around the dolls' house being built by her editor and publisher Norman Warne as a Christmas gift for his niece Winifred. Possibly the most famous dolls' house, is the one at Windsor Castle designed for Queen Mary in 1924 by the prominent architect, Sir Edwin Lutyens. At 5' tall, and containing 16 fully furnished rooms, it took 4 years to complete. It has working plumbing and lights and is filled with miniature forms of the finest and most modern goods of the period. Famous writers and artists contributed scale size books and framed artworks to decorate the rooms, while carpets were woven by Axminster and Wilton. A very grand house in miniature, very much in the style of its predecessors.

FEB 26TH - MARCH 4TH 1974

IN THE NEWS

Tuesday 26   **"Fear for Painting Grows"** A caller claiming to have stolen the Vermeer 'Elm' painting, said it would be destroyed unless £500,000 worth of food was flown to Grenada in the West Indies in 14 days. Further paintings will be stolen if the demand isn't met.

Wednesday 27   **"Fishy Business"** The Government is being asked to give financial support for a freezer trawler to explore for new types of fish, after a trawler landed a catch of 'unusual fish', which sold quickly at Fleetwood Market to big firms such as Birds Eye and Ross Fish.

Thursday 28   **"Election outcome hangs in balance"** British polls remained open until 10 pm in a watershed general election. It closed as one of the most inconclusive and confused stalemate general elections the United Kingdom has known.

Friday March 1   **"Royal Navy to Help"** 9 members of the Royal Navy will carry out bomb disposal work in the Suez Canal over the next 6 months. Explosives and 15 shipwrecks on the canal floor are from conflicts since 1967.

Saturday 2   **"Heathrow Strike"** British Airways cancelled 140 flights from Heathrow involving 5,000 passengers booked on Continental flights and almost 3,000 on domestic flights. 400 ground engineers are on strike.

Sunday 3   **"Major Wine Fraud"** Two leading French wine companies manufactured and sold wine made from dregs, sugar, glycerine and sulphuric acid in deals worth over 60m francs (£6m). A court heard the result *'tasted like wine but tended to upset the stomach'*.

Monday 4   **"New Government"** Mr Heath resigned, making way for a Labour Administration, and the Queen has asked Mr Harold Wilson to form a new government.

HERE IN BRITAIN

"Seaweed Hazard"

Volunteers are needed to help clear an invasive Japanese seaweed which threatens to choke the south coast of England. The fast-growing Sargassum Muticum weed, in Portsmouth harbour and on the Isle of Wight coast, is spreading rapidly, and could cause huge problems as it did on the Pacific coast of America, where it has clogged harbours and smothered valuable fishing grounds.

The weed which grows up to 20ft long at half an inch a day, was introduced accidentally into our seas - possibly in ships' bilge water or with oyster shipments.

AROUND THE WORLD

"The Bare Faced Cheek!"

The latest student craze to sweep America is midnight nude racing. The races, called 'streaking' take place under cover of darkness across the large campus areas of both universities and colleges, with institutions vying with each other to break records for the longest dash and the most nude runners.

Currently students at Western Carolina University hold the new national record of a 409-yard dash with 138 students, including 25 girls. This was run to support their demands for 24-hour visiting rights at all college dormitories and to allow beer sales on the campus.

SHROVE TUESDAY

This week held Shrove Tuesday, the day before Ash Wednesday, when people traditionally went to confession to be 'shriven' or absolved of their sins before the Lenten fast. A bell would be rung to call people to confession, which became known as the 'Pancake Bell' and is still rung today. Any foods which weren't allowed during the fast had to be eaten up by midnight on the Tuesday or thrown out. The eggs were made into pancakes on the Tuesday and from this developed the custom of holding Pancake Races.

It has been suggested that the origins of the tradition came from a housewife in Olney, Buckinghamshire in 1445. The woman had been so busy making pancakes that she lost track of time, which led to her running to church still carrying her frying pan when she heard the bells ringing to signal the 11am service. Olney is one of the many towns that still have the traditional Pancake Race held each Shrove Tuesday, and which was won this year by a schoolgirl, Sally Ann Faulkner.

But racing with a hot frying pan is only one of the traditional activities on this day. 'Old rules' football games, where the goals can be several miles, or villages apart, are still held in Alnwick and Sedgefield in the Northeast, Atherstone in Warwickshire, and Ashbourne in Derbyshire. The game is played with an indeterminate number of players, over an unspecified area, and there are no rules, whatsoever. It is certainly not a game for the faint hearted, and injuries are quite common. In Scarborough the day is known as 'Skipping Day' and everyone assembles on the promenade to skip. Long ropes are stretched across the road and there might be ten or more people skipping on one rope, girls and grown women together.

March 5th - 11th 1974

IN THE NEWS

Tuesday 5 "Cafe Royal Fined £50" The Cafe Royal in London was fined £75 for describing a dish on the menu as 'free range chicken in butter' when instead it was a battery hen.

Wednesday 6 "Ex-PC Cancelled Own Marriage" A former policeman decided to end his marriage by making a rubber stamp with the words "Registrar General, Somerset House, Cancellation of Marriage" to use on the certificate to indicate it was dissolved. His case continues at Winchester.

Thursday 7 "Miners' Leaders Accept New Pay Deal" Normal work at the pits will resume on Monday, following a vote of 25-2 by the executive of the miners' union, recommending its members to accept the latest pay settlement.

Friday 8 "Midlands Bread Shortage Spreads" A strike of delivery men has now spread to the East Midlands, causing a chaotic bread shortage across the centre of England, with rising prices and long queues.

Saturday 9 "The Oldest Man in Britain" The oldest man in Britain, a retired chemist from Harrogate, managed to celebrate his 110th birthday this week in his nursing home.

Sunday 10 "Shopkeepers Would Accept 5% Cut in Food Profits" Retailers have informed the Price Commission they will reluctantly accept a cut in food profit margins but only for six months. The commission had requested a 10% cut.

Monday 11 "Judge Gives Man Garden Access" A judge in Teignmouth, Devon, has ordered an estranged wife to allow her husband access to the garden of their house, so he can prevent it from getting overgrown. She had locked the garden gate to keep him out.

HERE IN BRITAIN

"Save The Village Pond"

A campaign was launched this week to save the rapidly disappearing village pond. Only 200,000 remain in the country, with up to 100 a week currently being lost. The statistics are alarming enough to make the campaign urgent and those who were not aware of the gravity of the situation, were given all the facts.

A 96-page book called Save the Village Pond is being published as part of the national campaign and a full-time advisory centre has been set up to assist village groups in preserving this feature of the countryside and wildlife habitat.

AROUND THE WORLD

"Heard after 3,700 Years"

The words of an ancient song written in cuneiform symbols, was discovered on thick clay tablets in the 50's by archaeologists on the Syrian coast, where the ancient Ugarit people lived from about 2000 to 600 BC.

Having finally been deciphered in 1972, it was heard again at the University of California this week. The oldest song, the in the world, which sounds to contemporary ears like a lullaby, a hymn or a gentle folk song was last heard, scholars said, about 1800 BC in the ancient Eastern city of Ugarit on the Mediterranean coast.

STAY IN A LANDMARK

A 19th century fort in the Channel Islands

The Landmark Trust is an organisation very much engaged in practical conservation and becoming increasingly popular. Founded in 1965 by a director of Coutts Bank who is a dedicated conservationist, its main aim is to preserve and restore buildings that would in different circumstances have become derelict or disappeared altogether. To do this it provides the opportunity for people who would otherwise be no more than day visitors to actually stay in historic buildings. *"To appreciate a place properly it is not enough to see it briefly by day"*, the trust's handbook says. *"It is essential to go to sleep there and wake up there and be there in all lights and weathers."*

Properties that can be rented for a weekend break, or even a week, vary from an 18th century Gothic temple at Stowe, or an Italianate Victorian railway station in North Staffordshire, to a 2 room cottage in Cardiganshire, or a 19th century fort in the Channel Islands. Although not the cheapest holiday rentals on the market, they must be reckoned good value when you consider how rents of holiday cottages on the commercial market have been increasing.

Electricity for cooking, heating, hot water and lighting is included, and all properties are sympathetically restored, with the fixtures and furnishings being of an exceptionally high standard. Many are set in picturesque rural surroundings or are part of the architectural landscape of interesting towns that would be greatly impoverished if they were to fall down or be demolished. Many are handsome minor buildings that contribute to the scene, and buildings and sites that may not be outstanding, but are key elements in a landscape or townscape. *"Buildings that fall through the preservation net "* is how the Landmark Trust describes them.

MARCH 12TH - 18TH 1974

IN THE NEWS

Tuesday 12 — **"Archbishop to Retire"** Dr. Michael Ramsay, the 100th Archbishop of Canterbury, has announced that he will retire on November 15th, after 13 years as head of the Church of England. He will receive a lifetime peerage.

Wednesday 13 — **"Fierce New Clashes"** Mrs Golda Meir, the Israeli Prime Minister, speaking from Tel Aviv, announced that the occupied Golan Heights had come under heavy Syrian artillery and tank fire for almost four hours.

Thursday 14 — **"Not Thirst Quenching"** Balmoral Castle's water supply contains dangerously high levels of lead according to experts. Victorian lead plumbing is probably the cause. Readings show 100 micrograms of lead compared to 10 in London and only 3 in Inverness.

Friday 15 — **"Clothes ON Please"** 30 people are to appear in court after rugby supporters fought and threw bottles at police at Piccadilly Circus. A man climbed to the top of traffic lights and started to undress while 15 policemen were controlling a crowd of about 800 Welsh supporters ahead of the International at Twickenham.

Saturday 16 — **"A Clean Sweep"** Members of the controversial Clay Cross Labour Party won six seats in the District Council election on Saturday. They showed solidarity with the 11 Labour councillors previously disqualified from office for defying the Housing Finance Act.

Sunday 17 — **"Military Parade"** The Queen Mother attended the St Patrick's Day parade at Caterham Barracks and was presented with a Shamrock corsage by the Commander-in-Chief of the United Kingdom Land Forces.

Monday 18 — **"Cell Bars Cut"** The Provisional IRA Littlejohn brothers escaped from Mountjoy prison, Dublin, where they were serving the longest sentences ever imposed in the Irish Republic. They were convicted for a £67,000 bank robbery.

HERE IN BRITAIN

"Moon Dust"

The British Steel Corporation is supporting work in the chemistry department of Bristol University to reproduce processes that might alter rocks on the moon's surface and could help to avoid corrosion of metals on Earth.

However, before the processes on the Moon and in the industrial workshop can be explored further, scientists need a new method of analysis for the special material which is still locked in the container in which it was brought back from the Moon.

AROUND THE WORLD

"Go to Work on an Egg"

Fifteen live hens were taken by helicopter from Kathmandu to a Himalayan base camp this week to help an attempt at the women's world mountaineering record. The leader of the Japanese team of 12 women, accompanied the hens as they were flown to the camp near the Manaslu peak in North-western Nepal.

"I hope they lay eggs at that altitude", she said. *"We need lots of eggs to fuel our efforts to climb this mountain."*

BRITISH SUMMER TIME

This year British Summer Time began at 2 am on Sunday, March 17th when clocks went forward an hour. British Summer Time was established by an act of parliament in 1916, following a campaign against the waste of working time on summer mornings. It was then adopted in the rest of the European countries involved in WW1.

The practice involved putting clocks forward by one hour in Spring, so that mornings had one hour less daylight, and evenings one hour more. Clocks were then put back one hour on the last Sunday in October and summertime ended. The length of the actual day did not alter but sunrise and sunset appeared to be an hour later. During WWII, in order to increase productivity in industry and agriculture, Britain used British Double Summertime, meaning that clocks were put forward by 2 hours during the summer, and in winter they were put back only one hour. From 1901-1936 King Edward VII operated a daylight-saving system at Sandringham because he loved hunting in winter. Therefore, all the clocks on the Norfolk estate were put forward by 30 minutes!

There have been many debates as to whether we should continue like this. In 1959 many wanted a permanent change to clocks going forward by one hour, and in 1966 the government introduced the British Standard Time Experiment, with clocks being one hour ahead all year before reverting to normal again. However, many farmers, as well as residents of Scotland and Northern Ireland, oppose doing away with British Summertime as it would mean that in some areas, the winter sunrise would be at 10:00am or even later, and school children would travel in the dark, on colder, icier roads, possibly leading to more accidents.

March 19th - 25th 1974

IN THE NEWS

Tuesday 19 — **"Bridge Streakers"** A woman aged 21 was among seven 'streakers' who brought traffic to a standstill yesterday as they dashed in the nude across Kingston Bridge, Surrey. The woman 'display artist' was later arrested.

Wednesday 20 — **"Kidnap Attempt "** Princess Anne and Captain Mark Phillips' car was blocked and several shots fired as they were returning to Buckingham Palace. They were unhurt, but their chauffeur and detective, a policeman and a passenger in a passing taxi were wounded.

Thursday 21 — **"Faster Travel"** A new rush-hour service from Northampton to London Euston has been introduced. Journey times will be reduced the by 20 minutes to less than an hour.

Friday 22 — **"Speeding Up"** Restrictions on petrol consumption are to be eased and the motorway speed limit will revert to 70 mph. However, on other roads the 50-mph limit will continue for the time being.

Saturday 23 — **"Mousetrap Move"** The best-selling Agatha Christie play, The Mousetrap, which has run for the last 21 years at the Ambassadors' Theatre, is to move and will reopen at St Martin's Theatre next door.

Sunday 24 — **"Place Your Bets Please"** Ladbrokes bookmakers are taking bets on who will be the next Archbishop of Canterbury. Among the favourites are the current Archbishop of York, Donald Coggan at 3-1, with long shots Trevor Huddleston and David Sheppard at 20-1.

Monday 25 — **"Cheerful Banter at Kremlin"** The three days of talks between Dr Henry Kissinger, the American Secretary of State and the Soviet leaders opened in a relaxed atmosphere tinged with a good-humoured informality that augured well for the future.

HERE IN BRITAIN

"Going, Going, Gone"

As one of our great stately homes, Chatsworth House contains many treasures. In a forthcoming sale at Christie's, several books and manuscripts from the 15th and 16th centuries will attract much attention.

An illuminated manuscript of Chaucer's Canterbury Tales, one of the rarest in existence, was written between 1440 and 1450 and family tradition has it that it was a wedding present for Margaret Beaufort, grandmother of King Henry VIII, and was bought by the sixth Duke of Devonshire for £357 in 1812. It is expected to make a handsome profit when the hammer comes down!

AROUND THE WORLD

"Lisbon Bottom Pinchers!"

A book by Portuguese authors 'The Three Marias', which has been condemned as pornographic literature, has been defended by a drama critic saying it is impossible for a woman to go around Lisbon without being insulted on the street.

As a defence witness in court, she stated that women in Lisbon are constantly grabbed and pinched and are a frequent target of insulting remarks and shocking proposals from young men. She criticised the attitude of upper-class Portuguese men saying they often try to use their social position to take advantage of girls from poorer backgrounds.

MOTHERING SUNDAY

This week will see frenzied activity in any shop selling chocolates, perfume or flowers, for this weekend sees the annual celebration of 'Mothers' Day', if you follow American tradition, or 'Mothering Sunday' if you prefer British tradition. But gone are the days when a simple bunch of flowers or a little box of chocolates were possible, now it is a case of bigger and better, and the same product that you find on the shelves throughout the year is re-packaged and dressed up to the nines, given added value and an excuse for at least a 100% mark up in price.

The celebration itself dates back to Medieval times when it was a welcome break from the rigours of the Lenten Fast, but it fell out of fashion until two ladies, on either side of the Atlantic decided to revive it at the beginning of the 20th century. Anna Maria Jarvis was the founder of Mothers' Day in America, when in 1908, three years after her mother's death, Jarvis held a memorial ceremony to honour her, marking the first official Mother's Day. Single carnations were the floral emblem, red carnations representing living mothers and the white carnation honouring deceased mothers.

By 1943, disillusioned with the growing commercialism associated with it, Anna began organising a petition to rescind Mother's Day. In England, Constance Adelaide Smith was inspired by a newspaper article about Anna Jarvis but linked the idea to the Mothering Sunday observed in the Anglican Church on the fourth Sunday of Lent. She established a movement to promote the day, collecting and publishing information about its traditional observance throughout Britain. By the time of her death, in 1938 the day was said to be observed in every parish in Britain, and every country in the British Empire.

March 26th - April 1st 1974

IN THE NEWS

Tuesday 26   **"Kicked Whilst he Was Down"** The Duke of Edinburgh was shaken and bruised when the carriage he was driving overturned. He was thrown to the ground and kicked by one of the horses.

Wednesday 27   **"Lady Chatterley Dispute"** The proposed name "Chatterley Mews" for a new street in Nottinghamshire has been rejected. The council chairman said, *"Lawrence was a great author, but as far as 'Lady Chatterley's Lover' is concerned, he was a dirty old man and a peeping Tom."*

Thursday 28   **"Weedkiller Lost"** Two containers containing paraquat weed killer were lost off the back of a lorry on a road near Peterborough. Police officers issued a warning that the one-gallon drums each contained enough poison to kill several hundred people.

Friday 29   **"Higher Benefits"** More than 11.5m people, pensioners and the disadvantaged, will benefit from the biggest increase in the new national insurance scheme.

Saturday 30   **"Museums Rejoice"** Multi coloured balloons flew from the flagstaff at the Tate Gallery in London to celebrate the abolition of admission charges at national museums and galleries. Visitor numbers dropped by 50% since charges began in January.

Sunday 31   **"Moon for Mercury"** The planet Mercury appears to have a moon of its own, the thirty-third discovered in the solar system. An ultraviolet device on board Mariner 10, the American spaceship, has detected a detached body in motion around the planet.

Monday 1   **"Spring Visitors"** A warm weekend meant busy roads, and full car parks as temperatures in the south hit the low 60's. Sea bathers near Christchurch were treated to the company of a school of porpoise only half a mile offshore.

HERE IN BRITAIN

"All Change"

England and Wales are now subject to the most radical reform of local government since the nineteenth century. Greater London, reformed 10 years ago, provides the model for the 6 metropolitan counties of Greater Manchester, Merseyside, South Yorkshire, Tyne and Wear, West Midlands, and West Yorkshire. The new system has not been easy to instigate, with existing and new authorities running in tandem, but as the dawn breaks on the new world of local government, one chief officer commented, *'At least now we can see the dark at the end of the tunnel.'*

AROUND THE WORLD

"Au Revoir"

The 'France', the biggest of the world's remaining elite transatlantic liners, is to retire. The 66,348-ton liner had been crippled by prohibitive running costs caused by the energy crisis. This sleek ship was the longest passenger vessel in the world when she was built in 1961 and could carry more than 2,000 passengers served by a crew of 1,000. She made her maiden voyage to New York in just over four days. Her main rivals were the Queen Mary, the Queen Elizabeth and the United States - all retired because of mass air travel.

RED RUM

Red Rum has become a household name after winning the 135th Grand National race at Aintree this weekend. The nine-year-old was bred at Rossenarra Stud in Kells, County Kilkenny, and trained by Ginger McCain at Southport. A thoroughbred steeple chaser, he was suffering from an incurable bone disease when ex-second-hand car dealer McCain bought him for his client Noël le Mare, for 6,000 guineas in 1972. As part of his training programme, he was regularly ridden through the sea off Southport which may have been crucial in alleviating his condition, and the rest, as they say, is history.

The Aintree course, which is shaped like an irregular triangle, must be run twice to cover the 4.5 miles and 30 jumps, including the notorious and hazardous Becher's and Valentine's Brooks. Being a handicap race also means that the horses must have immense stamina and strength to cope with heavier jockeys and challenging jumps over such a distance. However Red Rum not only took all these in his stride, but beat the Cheltenham Gold Cup winner, L'Escargot, by an impressive 7 lengths. This is Red Rum's second consecutive year as National winner, making him one of only six horses to win twice since 1837.

The run was not without its faults however, as on the second lap, he stumbled at the fifth fence, but recovered instantly and carried on effortlessly with no further problems. Ridden by Brian Fletcher who on Saturday repeated last year's victory, admitted that he was concerned that Red Rum was carrying his 12st weight over the gruelling course, but said, *"I had to let him stride on, as he was going so well and freely, but apart from that small mistake he gave me the winning feel all the way. What a horse!"*

April 2ND - 8TH 1974

IN THE NEWS

Tuesday 2 — **"Women Jockeys Beat the Men"** Named as "The Lads and Lassies Handicap", the first ever mixed flat race at Nottingham saw women jockeys triumphing over the men.

Wednesday 3 — **"President Dies Suddenly"** The French President, Georges Pompidou, died suddenly and news broadcast on radio and television struck France like a thunderbolt. The immediate reaction was one of consternation and anxiety as to what the future held in store, as the whole of French political life was centred in the head of state.

Thursday 4 — **"The Mysterious Signature"** Scotland Yard are investigating the mystery of Prime Minister Harold Wilson's forged signature on three 'land deal' business documents involving three close friends of the Premier.

Friday 5 — **"Contraceptives for All Teenagers"** A sex education consultant has said that contraceptive information and supplies should be available to all teenagers. Parents should get the support of the family doctor to ensure their teenage children could seek help in confidence.

Saturday 6 — **"Workers Sound of Silence"** The members of the Association of Scientific, Technical and Managerial Staff have taken a vow of silence in their fight for a week's extra holiday.

Sunday 7 — **"Bullies Face a Clean-up in The Kitchen"** With an increasing number of classroom assaults on teachers a Tory councillor has advocated an alternative punishment to writing out lines. He suggests making offenders do the school's washing up after lunch instead.

Monday 8 — **"Danes Let Man Marry Niece"** An uncle of 26 and his 24-year-old niece whose marriage was annulled three years ago were married again today in Copenhagen at a civic ceremony. They already have two young children.

HERE IN BRITAIN

"Stop That Noise"

Dr Hugh Campbell, a government industrial adviser and scientist, was fined £75 after admitting damaging a generator belonging to a German television crew who were shooting scenes in St Giles's churchyard in the Barbican.
Dr Campbell, who had been entertaining friends to lunch, was finding it hard to hear the conversation and politely asked the crew to stop making so much noise. He was told rather curtly that they would be shooting for another half an hour, so he picked up the portable generator and threw it into the nearby ornamental lake.

AROUND THE WORLD

"Stricken QE2"

1,642 passengers were transferred from the crippled QE2 onto a Norwegian liner in heavy seas 250 miles off the Bermudan coast. The Sea Venture brought repair men, fuel for the emergency generator, and 20 cases of tinned food and drink for the crew.
The passengers praised the QE2 staff. *'They treated us very well'* said one, *'there was plenty of Scotch and Bourbon.'* One lady however said she had no complaints, but after the breakdown of the plumbing system on the QE2 she felt like *'spending the next six years in a bathtub.'*

WORLD BOOK DAY

INTERNATIONAL CHILDREN'S BOOK DAY

International Children's Book Day is celebrated around Hans Christian Andersen's birthday on 2nd April. Its purpose is to remind people of the importance of books to children, to draw attention to the shortage of books for the young in developing countries and to encourage support for a UNESCO Programme, which assists educational projects in many parts of the world. This year's slogan was 'Stories are wings that help you soar every day' and was marked with a literary pilgrimage made up of bibliophiles of all ages round the City of London, visiting buildings associated with authors who have written for children.

A halt was made at each place and the poem or piece of prose was recited. Unsuspecting passers-by were seen quickening their steps, but many were invited to join in the activities, such as when 'Ring-a-ring o' roses' was danced outside Guildhall, or 'London Bridge Is Falling Down' beside the site of the old London Bridge. Some did so reluctantly, but others gladly joined in with the spirit of childish enjoyment.

The 'Pied Piper' leading the enthusiastic parade was a lecturer at the Ealing School of Librarianship. The poem 'Macavity' was recited outside the basement of T.S.Eliot's workplace, Lloyds Bank, on Lombard Street, while Keats's 'La Belle Dame Sans Merci' was read in Cheapside, the area where he once lived. Cornhill was the birthplace of Thomas Gray, so his 'Elegy Written in A Country Churchyard' was read out beside Simpson's Tavern and at the corner of Wood Street and Cheapside, which Wordsworth mentioned in his poem 'Poor Susan', a thrush joined the voices and sang loudly in the old plane tree. Then outside St Vedast-alias-Foster Church in the City of London, where Herrick was christened, his 'Fair daffodils' made a show of gold in the churchyard.

April 9th – 15th 1974

IN THE NEWS

Tuesday 9 — **"Arms Shipment at Southampton"** Police found arms, including pistols, rifles, detonators and explosives at the bottom of a shipping container unloaded at Southampton, believed to be destined for Northern Ireland.

Wednesday 10 — **"Maiden Speech"** Princess Margaret and her son, Lord Linley were in the gallery to hear Lord Snowdon make his maiden speech after 12 years as a member of the House of Lords.

Thursday 11 — **"Compensation Suggested"** The Noise Advisory Council advocates that air traffic continue to fly over sparsely populated areas where possible, but suggested compensation for people in the noisiest areas, and stricter criteria to be applied to urban planning near airports.

Friday 12 — **"Rough and Tumble"** The brown bear cubs, born on January 9, were on view at London Zoo with their mother, Zookie, this week. Their father, Nikki, was born in captivity at Moscow Zoo.

Saturday 13 — **"Sent Home to Cool Off"** Twenty-seven crew men from a North Sea oil rig were taken ashore by helicopter after starting an industrial dispute over working hours.

Sunday 14 — **"State Grant for Genoese Silver"** Rare Genoese 16th century silver has been purchased by the Victoria and Albert Museum, with the aid of a government grant of £20,000. The ewer and dish are now on display inside the main entrance.

Monday 15 — **"Motorists Urged to Fill Up"** Roads were congested over the weekend, as people drove to the coast and favoured beauty spots for Easter. However, as supplies are still limited, motoring organisations urged motorists to ensure they had enough petrol to get home.

HERE IN BRITAIN

"The Race Goes On"

The Scot, Chay Blyth, brought his boat, the huge 'Great Britain II', home first this week but the battle for the overall winner of the Whitbread-sponsored 'Round the World Race' is still undecided. After seven months of punishing sailing, the likely winner, the Mexican owned yacht 'Sayula' has three and a half days to make up 160 miles which separates her from the Royal Navy entry, 'Adventure'.

Normally, this would be an easy task, but race control reported that Ramon Carlin and his international crew have managed to get *'their ropes and sails all tangled up'*!

AROUND THE WORLD

"The Naval Salute That Misfired"

The Royal Navy's ice patrol ship, Endurance, was en route home after her winter in the Antarctic, when she stood by off Cape Horn to see the Round the World Yacht Race fleet safely round the notorious South American headland.

She fired a nine-gun salute for the Navy's own entry, the 'Adventure', but there was consternation on her bridge when the sixth shot, although a blank, made a hole in the ocean racer's head sail, which the crew spent the rest of the day sewing up. *"Visibility was bad, and the sea was rough"* the captain reported.

MAUNDY MONEY

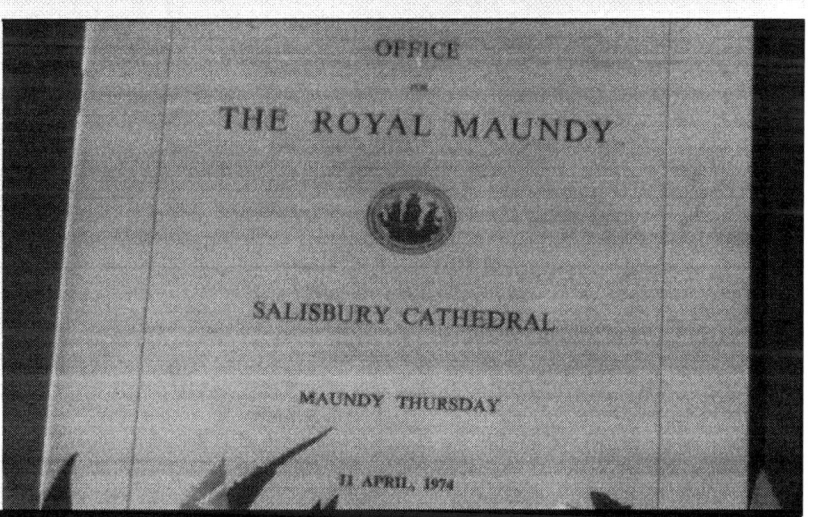

The Royal Maundy ceremony of 1877

The distribution of Maundy Money, which takes place on the Thursday before Easter, is the modern development of an ancient ceremony said to be derived from when Christ washed his disciples' feet the evening before his crucifixion. In Britain the service goes back many centuries and Elizabeth I personally took part in 1572, in the hall at Greenwich. On that occasion a laundress, the sub-Almoner and the Lord High Almoner washed the feet of the poor people, and the feet then being, apparently, thoroughly clean, were again washed and kissed by the Queen herself. She then distributed broadcloth for the making of clothes and fish, bread and wine. Royalty continued to take part but the last time the foot-washing ritual took place was in 1685. Several changes have taken place since then. Clothing was substituted for broadcloth for the women but that was stopped in 1724 and money was given in lieu. In 1837 William IV agreed to give the pensioners thirty shillings in lieu of all provisions.

For many years the ceremony took place in Whitehall Chapel moving later to Westminster Abbey. Today, the service is held in various cathedrals, Salisbury this year, and the Queen has personally distributed her royal gift almost every year since her coronation. In addition to banknotes and cash (including a crown piece) which have now taken the place of all other forms of gift, the pensioners receive some of the world's most interesting coins presented in a small leather purse, with as many pence as the monarch has years of age. The recipients themselves number as many men and as many women as the monarch has years. In the days before base metal money, the amount was made up from silver pennies, twopences, threepences and fourpences and are still, today, struck in silver and polished like proof coins.

April 16th – 22nd 1974

IN THE NEWS

Tuesday 16   **"Motorway Pile-Up"** Children are believed to have set fire to a grass embankment alongside the M62 near Wakefield, Yorkshire, and caused a nine-car collision. Thick smoke covered part of the motorway's eastbound carriageway and two cars collided as they entered the area. Others piled into them.

Wednesday 17   **"Chinese Invitation"** Harold Wilson has received an invitation from the Vice-premier to visit China. However, the political pressure in Britain might make an early visit difficult.

Thursday 18   **"Cash for Scots Newspaper"** More than 600 redundant newspaper workers were asked to invest £400 each in a daily newspaper to be produced in the former Scottish Daily Express building in Glasgow.

Friday 19   **"Protest by Women"** About 50 women converged on the London Passport Office demanding to have "Ms" put on their passports instead of "Miss" or "Mrs".

Saturday 20   **"Tomatoes 10p a Pound Cheaper After Easter"** Tomatoes have been the centre of controversy in the past fortnight when prices rose in the week before Easter. The cause, according to the Consumer Council, was not profiteering but a strong demand for salad vegetables during the holiday period.

Sunday 21   **"Census Form Tests"** A new census form is being trialled in various parts of the country aiming to streamline the next questionnaire in 1981. The prototype form contains 50% fewer questions.

Monday 22   **"£500 Offered for Return Of Television Cat"** Arthur, the famous white cat loved by millions, who uses his paw to eat his supper straight out of the Kattomeat tin, was abducted from his home in Essex and £250 is being offered for his safe return.

HERE IN BRITAIN

"The Year of the Beard"

According to the National Hairdressers' Federation, this is the year of the beard. The President described *'the hairy revolution that has crept upon the jowls of the British male'*. He wondered whether the new trend followed an admiration for Victorian fashion. If so, the federation members would have to freshen up on how to achieve 'Imperials', 'Van Dykes', 'mutton chops', 'spades', 'Uncle Sams', 'Dundrearies' and 'Piccadilly Weepers' *'where the hair left the head in a horizontally outward direction'*

AROUND THE WORLD

"Sleepless in Dubrovnik"

Dubrovnik is now one of the world's most fashionable tourist spots with increasing numbers travelling to enjoy the breath-taking scenery and architectural splendour of this medieval maritime city.
However the holidaymakers are complaining that they cannot sleep at night because of the noise of flights from Cilipi Airport, transporting even more holidaymakers! It has been decided therefore to operate a total curfew and close Dubrovnik's airport between 22.00 and 06.00, so that tourists can get a *'peaceful sleep'*.

THE WAY FORWARD

The Ordnance Survey have been leading the way since 1791 when mapping the South coast became a top priority as Britain prepared for war against Napoleon. During the 19th century more of the English landscape was mapped, copies proving popular despite being expensive to produce, because they offered a bird's eye view of the landscape – until then only the privilege of hot air balloonists. The 20th century brought more cyclists and motorists onto the roads and ramblers into the countryside and there was potential for huge map sales among this expanding leisure market.

In 1972 the first Outdoor Leisure Map was published with more popular areas being mapped to provide the remainder of this national series called 'Pathfinder'. However, a problem has arisen in the latest series of maps which the British Mountaineering Council considers is an 'error' by the cartographers likely to lead to accidents. The dotted lines indicating footpaths are too similar to those for the new district council boundaries. For example, on the new Snowdonia map the boundary line runs parallel with the footpath along the summit ridge of Carnedd Llywelyn and then diverges as the path continues Northeast, while the boundary line drops over Black Ladder Cliffs.

The problem is that the traditional black dashed line used for a footpath has been used in a slightly bolder form for the boundary lines, leaving room for error. The cartographers will take another look to see if matters are confused, but any changes would be costly as thousands of these maps have been printed. The head of the Snowdonia Mountain Rescue Team commented that *'the mountaineers had got a little hysterical. A simple label or addendum might be useful on the map, but most of the footpaths were well marked.'*

APRIL 23RD - 29TH 1974

IN THE NEWS

Tuesday 23 — **"Skates Win Awards "** A Slough firm has been nominated for the Queen's Awards to Industry this week. They doubled sales last year to over £600,000 worth of premium skates for export to Canada and Russia.

Wednesday 24 — **"Bud Abbott Dies "** Bud Abbott, straight man in the 1940s film comedy duo, Abbott and Costello, died at Woodlands Hills, California at the age of 75. His partner Lou Costello died in 1959.

Thursday 25 " — **Wireless Pioneer"** The centenary of the birth of Marconi is being marked with a special exhibition at the Science Museum. In a new biography, the inventor is described as *'a dreamy, ignorant youth with what seemed to be a presumptuous, half- baked ambition'*.

Friday 26 — **"Anonymous Hazard"** An Australian sociologist argues that the anonymity of the motorist encourages irresponsible and aggressive driving which would be reduced if drivers' names were displayed on the sides of their vehicles.

Saturday 27 — **"The Romance is Over"** Prince Charles, back from four months duty on HMS Jupiter, has not seen Lady Jane Wellesley, his companion for the past 18 months and they will not visit Badminton together as expected.

Sunday 28 — **"Australia's New Anthem"** About 150 campaigners who are vehemently against the new national anthem 'Advance Australia Fair', sang 'God Save The Queen' instead at a concert in Melbourne.

Monday 29 — **"Man Threatens to Sue the Queen"** A man who runs a donkey sanctuary in Surrey has objected to the way the Queen and Capt. Mark Phillips rode at Badminton, saying they rode in a way that *'contravened the Protection of Animals Act, 1911.'*

HERE IN BRITAIN

"Football Hooligans"

Hooliganism among Manchester United supporters is to be investigated by the Minister of State for Sport. The referee abandoned Saturday's game five minutes before the end, with Manchester City leading 1-0, and Manchester United relegated to the Second Division.

Hundreds of spectators ran on to the pitch after the goal was scored and a fire began behind the Manchester City goal and supporters came back on to the pitch. The Minister said, *'We cannot allow fans to stop a game in the belief that it will automatically be replayed'.*

AROUND THE WORLD

"A Symbol Of Hope"

Britain's sailors have begun the dangerous task of clearing the Suez Canal of bombs and mines as one of the first steps in Egypt's canal reconstruction plan as they resurrect the city now that the 'Suez affair' belongs to the past. Already the fruits of the Navy's mission are to be seen.

This week the three mine-hunters Wilton, Maxton and Gossington completed the clearance of Port Said harbour and the canal's entrance. After seven years in which one of the world's busiest ports became a dead city, Egypt will be able to declare it open for business again.

WOMEN IN THE POLICE

Shirley Becke (top) and some of the first female police officers (below).

The first woman commander in the Metropolitan Police Force, Shirley Becke, retired this week after 33 years as a policewoman. During that time the role of women has changed beyond all recognition. The first female police constables were a voluntary force which operated in the cities of Bath and Bristol in the early 20th century. They were assisted by male officers but involved themselves solely with cases which involved women. The idea spread to all the major cities in Britain, and numbers in the force increased until after WWI when the government's policy was to reduce the number of women in paid employment.

Mrs Becke joined the police in 1941, having previously been the first woman to train as a gas engineer. She wanted to do her bit for the war effort and had heard there was a serious shortage of police. In those days there were fewer than a hundred policewomen, compared with about 650 today. After only four weeks' basic training she was posted to West End Central as a constable in uniform. The beat around Piccadilly Circus was a maelstrom of troops from all over the world, black marketeers, prostitutes and pimps, the Blitz, Civil Defence, and assorted crime, but women were seen mainly as clerical or minor incident support personnel well into the 60's.

Until then, although a few women were allowed to join CID, they were only allowed to handle 'soft' cases, such as shoplifting, or taking statements from women who had been sexually assaulted, or sometimes theft - provided the offence had been committed in a women's lavatory. Until recent times, male and female police staff were segregated, having separate ranks, duties and sometimes facilities as well. The situation changed in the 1970s, when the Equal Pay Act was finally introduced.

April 30th - May 6th 1974

IN THE NEWS

Tuesday 30   **"Call for Boycott"** The African Council for Sport has appealed to Britain to cancel the British Lions rugby tour of South Africa next month. They say a total boycott of South Africa is essential to combat racial discrimination in sport.

Wednesday 1   **"Danish State Visit"** The Queen of Denmark and The Prince of Denmark arrived for a State Visit. They were driven by carriage to Windsor Castle accompanied by The Queen and The Duke of Edinburgh.

Thursday 2   **"Sir Alf Ramsey Sacked"** Ramsey's 11-year reign as England's manager has ended. After elimination from the World Cup in 1970 and again this year, he has been criticised for being too cautious.

Friday 3   **"Life Beyond Earth"** The Royal Society have concluded that earthbound men have not established contact with intelligent life elsewhere, not because Homo sapiens is not clever enough but because the nearest intelligent life could be several light years away.

Saturday 4   **"Summer Exhibition"** The Royal Academy's 206th Summer Exhibition at Burlington House was opened with a private view for invited guests. The reviews varied, as did the work, and some critics dubbed it only 'mediocre'.

Sunday 5   **"Ronnie to Come Home"** Ronald Biggs, the train robber, is to be extradited after all. He will be flown out of Brazil this week.

Monday 6   **"Electrified Line"** The 400-mile train journey from London to Glasgow now takes five rather than six hours. The electrified part of Britain's railway network is now 17% of the whole. Electric locomotives are cheaper to buy, maintain and run, quieter and cleaner than diesel.

HERE IN BRITAIN

"London to Brighton"

On the 2nd Sunday in May each year, a cavalcade of old commercial vehicles slowly leaves London heading for Brighton, on the long-established run started back in 1958 by the Historic Commercial Vehicles Society.

Neat little delivery vans with gleaming chrome and corporate colours, and old lorries with hand painted signage, move at the stately pace of 20 mph, alongside WWI ambulances and police vans. This year there was even a 1925 Swedish fire engine. They are a reminder of when urban motoring was possibly more of a pleasure than a chore.

AROUND THE WORLD

"Karate Blow on Football Star"

During a friendly international football match in Sydney between Australia and Uruguay, the Australian centre forward, Ray Baartz, was felled by a blow from Uruguay's Luis Garisto.

The team doctor reported that the injury, which left Baartz paralysed on his left side and with his vision also affected, was, in his view, made by a karate blow to the throat, typically designed to kill an opponent.

After Baartz had been taken off the field, the teams played on and Australia, in spite of being a man down, went on to victory, beating Uruguay.

MAY DAY TRADITIONS

A wheel of cheese in the Randwick Wap ceremony (inset) and Maypole dancing (main).

May Day is a celebration of spring and many of the associated festivities date back to early Medieval times. The 1st of May was traditionally the start of 'Mary's Month' or a month of Christian devotions to the Virgin Mary and was usually declared a holiday allowing everyone to enjoy their inevitable local fair and festivities.

At Oxford's Magdalen Bridge, crowds still gather at first light to hear the May Singing of a hymn, and a madrigal by the choristers of Magdalen College. Later in the day, local Morris dancers entertain those out and about in the city's main streets. In the Gloucestershire village of Randwick, an ancient ceremony known as the Randwick Wap dates back to the 14th century. The Wap is a fair, with a rowdy procession in costume. Three wheels of cheese are elaborately decorated and carried in the procession before being rolled three times round the churchyard. It is an occasion for much quaffing of ale and wine, and although banned in the Victorian period as 'too rowdy and boozy' it was enthusiastically revived two years ago.

Central to most May Day celebrations is the Maypole, which at one time was a large tree in the forest that was decorated in situ, but later was cut down and brought into the village to be decorated with flowers, wreaths, handkerchiefs and ribbons. Complicated dances are performed around it while holding the ribbons attached to the top, which then weave a colourful braid pattern down the length of the pole. During the 16th and 17th centuries, many of the famous village maypoles were destroyed and the celebrations banned as being 'occasions of sin'. However, the late 19th century saw a renewed interest in English customs and May Day became a fixture in the calendar once more.

May 7th - May 13th 1974

IN THE NEWS

Tuesday 7 — "Goldwyn Studios Go Up In Flames" Three months after the death of the film pioneer Samuel Goldwyn, fire has totally destroyed his famous Goldwyn Studios in Hollywood.

Wednesday 8 — "50 Mile Ban On Former Husband" A Yorkshire painter and decorator who has been jailed 6 times in the last 4 years for molesting his former wife, was 'told to catch the next train to Sheffield' and not to go within 50 miles of the marital home.

Thursday 9 — "Pollution Of The Rhine" The Dutch Minister for Public Health said that pollution levels of the River Rhine in Holland have reached a point where it poses a threat to all who depend on it, and a clean up operation is urgently needed.

Friday 10 — "Country's First Ecological Housing Society" A housing development in Hertfordshire that incorporates low energy features such as recycling facilities and solar heating will cost the same to build, but running costs will be much cheaper than normal housing.

Saturday 11 — "Film Hot Line" Six clergymen in Reading are to operate an evening telephone 'hot line' for people who are disturbed and upset after seeing the film 'The Exorcist' when it opens.

Sunday 12 — "Minister With A Mission" A Methodist minister in Oldham, Lancashire, and former missionary in China, is opening his house to the public, where they can view many Oriental items and memorabilia from his years of mission work out there.

Monday 13 — "Mr. Nixon Will Face Trial Rather Than Quit ' Impeached President Nixon faces increasing demand for his resignation, but is still reiterating that he will stay in office until found guilty in a trial by the Senate.

HERE IN BRITAIN

"Charing Cross Hospital"

Opened in the 19th century, the West London Infirmary with only 12 beds, was renamed Charing Cross Hospital. During WWI the hospital was well placed to receive the thousands of injured servicemen coming back to Britain from the fronts, being situated in the heart of central London and near to Charing Cross Station.

In the 1930's it was obvious that much larger premises were needed, but due to WWII, rebuilding on the site of the Fulham Hospital was delayed. The last patients were treated in 1973, and the buildings have now become a shelter for the homeless.

AROUND THE WORLD

"Work Begins On Lenin's Tomb"

Work was carried out in Red Square this week on the mausoleum housing Lenin's remains. The mausoleum was built in 1930 to house the tomb of Soviet Leader Vladimir Lenin.

Apart from closures in wartime, the preserved body, in a glass sarcophagus has been on almost continuous display since his death in 1924. It is re-embalmed every year, and the skin frequently treated with chemicals to maintain an unblemished appearance.

Many visitors still queue to view the body, but photography and filming are forbidden, as is talking, smoking, keeping hands in pockets or wearing hats.

ELEPHANT FAMILY TREE

It has long been understood that the elephants that we are familiar with in our zoos and on wildlife programmes, are descended from the much larger woolly mammoth. But in the intervening years between the two, lay a large grey area of unknown evolution. Until recently that is. An incredible piece of scientific detective work by the Animal Breeding Research Organisation in Edinburgh has revealed that the pre-historic and the modern animals, unlike other species, are probably separated more by geography rather than time.

Usually, when scientists try to reconstruct extinct animals, such as the dinosaurs, all they have to go on are a few pieces of fossilised bone. However, although the woolly mammoth became extinct about 10 thousand years ago, virtually complete specimens still turn up in the frozen wastes of Siberia. It was from such frozen remains that samples of mammoth skin and hair were obtained and compared with those of living elephants. Using pieces of skin and hair from one of these discoveries scientists have discovered that the mammoth's ancestors were probably smooth-skinned like the modern elephants of India and Africa today.

Elephants are adapted for a hot climate but they do however, possess a thin coat of hairs similar in nature to the coat of the mammoth even though the elephant is bald by comparison. But while the elephants were evolving in the tropics, another group of the species moved to colder regions, and developed a thick shaggy hair covering to survive the extreme cold. The mammoth's thick hairy coat was therefore a sophisticated adaptation to a cold climate. This idea fits in very well with the theory that more than a million year ago there were large elephant like mammals living in the warm latitudes that were the ancestors of both groups.

May 14th - 20th 1974

IN THE NEWS

Tuesday 14 — **"Children in Need"** As 'World In Action's' controversial television programme on adoption and fostering entered its final moments last night, 20 specially installed telephones in a London hotel started to ring with calls from 1600 viewers spurred into action to find out more about adoption and long and short-term fostering.

Wednesday 15 — **"Dr Coggan to Canterbury"** Following the resignation of Dr Michael Ramsey in November, the Archbishop of York, Dr Donald Coggan, is to be the next Archbishop of Canterbury and leader of the world's Anglican Church.

Thursday 16 — **"No Saturday Deliveries"** In a ballot this week, postmen voted overwhelmingly in favour of no more Saturday deliveries and a 5-day working week. They say the Post Office is short of staff because of low pay and long hours.

Friday 17 — **"Hanratty Inquiry"** There is mounting pressure to open an enquiry into a possible miscarriage of justice in the case of the A6 murder, for which James Hanratty was hanged. The MPs say there is new evidence that was not produced at the trial.

Saturday 18 — **"Say 'No' to the Bolshoi"** Equity, the actors' union, have made another attempt to stop the forthcoming visit of the Bolshoi Ballet, in protest over the Russians' treatment of the former Kirov Ballet dancers Valery and Galina Panov.

Sunday 19 — **"Back Home"** Racing driver Stirling Moss returned safely to London after being stranded for two days in the Sahara Desert because of an error in the navigation notes during the London-Sahara-Munich World Cup Rally.

Monday 20 — **"Bomb Blast at Heathrow"** An American traveller sustained the only injury but 50 cars were written off when a 100lb bomb exploded in a multi storey car park outside the Terminal One building at Heathrow Airport.

HERE IN BRITAIN

"Brotherhood of the Brave"

A reunion of heroes took place when members of the Victoria Cross and George Cross Association gathered from all over the world in London this week for their biennial reunion.

What unites them, apart from their bravery and medals, is their overwhelming modesty and reluctance to talk about the days of fire and death when they won their awards.

A party at the RAF club was followed the next day with a service at St-Martin-in-the-Fields, lunch at Chelsea Barracks and a reception with the Queen.

AROUND THE WORLD

"Crossword Ballot Paper"

Australian voters are facing a complicated federal election, where voting for the Senate, the House of Representatives and four referendum proposals to alter the constitution, could take up to 15 minutes for each voter.

They must mark every square in their papers in order of preference, a daunting task in New South Wales, where there are 73 candidates for the Senate!

The Prime Minister said, *'Do not be unduly hurried or hustled. Check that you have numbered every square in sequence.'*

JEWELS IN THE WHITE HOUSE

The White House dirty laundry continues to be washed in public thanks to an American society columnist who has been digging into the not so small matter of Patricia Nixon's jewels. Some of these are gifts from Saudi Arabian princes and other foreign heads of state, as well as Saudi gifts of jewels for the Nixon daughters, all of which were apparently undisclosed as such to the White House Gift Office, which keeps a close record of such matters.

The worst seeming aspect is that the jewels, previously worn in public, were transferred from Mrs Nixon's personal safe in her bedroom to the Gift Office, only after questions were raised about who owns them, and the reason given for the oversight in protocol was due to her *'secretary getting confused over some of the Saudi names'*. United States law forbids American officials or their relatives accepting gifts *"from any king, prince or foreign state"*. Although some were given as long ago as 1969, apparently the gift office and protocol officials knew nothing about them. Mrs Nixon's aides have said it was always her intention to give them to the national archives, indignantly asserting that she had never intended keeping the jewels after the President leaves office.

According to the magazine article, the gifts included a matched set of emeralds and diamonds in the form of necklace, bracelet, earrings, ring and brooch for which the White House had inexplicably obtained a valuation of $52,000 (about £21,600). The gift had been presented to Mr Nixon in 1969. Legal counsel to the President has said *"the Saudi jewels were not technically state gifts"*, and that *"nothing was said publicly because the donors might consider disclosure, or personal gifts winding up in a public depository, an insult."*

May 21st - 27th 1974

IN THE NEWS

Tuesday 21 — **"Stamps Going Up Again"** The Post Office warns that increases in postal and telephone charges will be coming next year. This is in addition to the increased cost next month to 4½p for first-class and 3½p for second-class mail.

Wednesday 22 — **"English Test For Doctors"** Tests designed to establish how fluent immigrant doctors are in written and spoken English, as well as to determine their competence to practice in our country, will be introduced next January.

Thursday 23 — **"Kidnapper Hospitalised"** The man who shot four people in an attempt to kidnap Princess Anne and hold her for a £3m ransom, was committed at the Central Criminal Court to a mental hospital. The attack, the first attempt to kidnap a member of the Royal Family, took place in The Mall in March.

Friday 24 — **"Vulcan Fright"** There were panic calls to the Ministry of Defence when an RAF Vulcan bomber flew over the city practising for the Queen's birthday fly-past. Despite flying at 1000 feet, many thought it was lower and about to crash.

Saturday 25 — **"Devon Breeds"** Devon's two native breeds of cattle, the Devons and South Devons, have generated interest amongst breeders from the French towns of Caen and Morlaix which could lead to increased EEC interest in UK cattle for breeding.

Sunday 26 — **"Man Charged After Van Hits Palace Gate"** A drunk driver caused havoc in Fleet Street when his Ford van seriously damaged four newspaper offices, before finally crashing into the gates of Buckingham Palace.

Monday 27 — **"BBC Strike Stops 'Live' Sport"** All "live" Bank holiday sports coverage on BBC Television today has been cancelled because of a strike by members of the National Association of Theatrical Television and Cine Employees.

HERE IN BRITAIN

"Cornish Revival"

The Cornish parliament met this week under the black and white flag of the ancient kingdom of Cornwall for the first time since 1753. The Stannary Parliament was originally formed to serve the interests of the tin miners, but now has a new following who want it to be revived to look after Cornish interests. The Queen and the Prime Minister were invited but wrote to say they could not attend. That was just as well, because the parliament's clerk did not book Lostwithiel Guildhall, and the parliament held its first session in a public house.

AROUND THE WORLD

"Blizzards And Rainstorms"

South-eastern areas of Australia have suffered the worst storms for years, with blizzards, torrential rain and gale force winds disrupting services and power. New South Wales was the worst state hit.

The wild weather and the 10ft waves which struck Sydney did widespread damage to homes bordering the waterfront and to yachts and boats in the harbour. The coastguard and RAAF helicopters rescued crew members from a Norwegian bulk carrier and another cargo ship, both of which ran aground and broke up.

WHIT WALKS

This week, Whit Sunday was celebrated around the world by Catholics, Anglicans and Methodists. This special day is celebrated to commemorate the descent of the Holy Spirit upon Christ's disciples and is the seventh day after Easter or Pentecost, its name deriving from the Anglo-Saxon word 'wit' meaning 'understanding' to celebrate the disciples being filled with the wisdom of the Holy Spirit.

Whit Monday was officially recognised as a bank holiday in 1871 and the day has a special cultural significance in the north west of England. Many workplaces including factories and cotton mills closed for the whole Whitsuntide week giving workers a holiday and towns held fairs, markets, and parades. Still, a major tradition is the 'Whit Walk' when local churches or chapels employ bands to lead traditional processions through the streets. The origin of these processions dates back to July 1821 when the children of Manchester commemorated the coronation of George IV and children of all denominations walked in procession from their schools and assembled at Ardwick Green to sing 'God Save the King'.

The Bradford Whit Walk has been held continuously since 1903 and is one of the most popular events on the race-walking calendar, attracting hundreds of entries. At the height of its popularity, it attracted top British race walkers and in the 20s and 30s was recognised as the breeding ground for British Olympians, with winners Tommy Green and Harold Whitlock going on to win Olympic gold medals in 1932 and 1936 respectively. This is also the week for many local brass band contests and workers to take the opportunity to enjoy canal boat rides, go to the races and of course, go to the seaside.

May 28th - June 3rd 1974

IN THE NEWS

Tuesday 28 — **"Ulster Shutdown"** The Army's takeover of 21 petrol stations and two oil storage depots in Northern Ireland brought swift retaliation from the organisers of the general strike in the province. The council's 'coordinating committee' said that all gas, power station and oil supply workers would cease work by midnight and that milk and bread supplies would be *'the responsibility of the Army'.*

Wednesday 29 — **"Friesian Champion"** The biggest cattle prize-winner at the Bath and West Show was a nine-year-old Friesian, 'Sharcombe Reflection Beth', bred in Canada and bought three years ago for £10,000.

Thursday 30 — **"Direct Rule for Ulster"** Westminster has once again brought Northern Ireland under direct rule for the next four months. This follows the resignation of Mr Brian Faulkner and the Unionist party.

Friday 31 — **"Queen Pays Tribute"** The Queen has paid tribute to the Metropolitan Police saying they do a vital and often dangerous job. She took the opportunity to thank the force for helping to prevent the kidnapping of Princess Anne in March.

Saturday 1 — **"28 People Killed"** A break in a main pipeline may have caused the major explosion at the Nypro chemical plant at Flixborough, on Humberside, where 28 people died.

Sunday 2 — **"Earlier Diagnosis of Cancer"** A ground-breaking method of making an early cancer diagnosis has been developed jointly by Cancer Research and the Royal Marsden Hospital. It uses an ultrasonic method to obtain shaded pictures from echo patterns.

Monday 3 — **"The London Pollen Count Starts"** The Asthma Research Council is to issue daily pollen counts to newspapers, radio, television and the telephone service in London and the Home Counties.

HERE IN BRITAIN

"Early Risers"

Since 1933 a 'dawn watch' study by the World Bird Research Station in Northumberland has charted the passage of birds in the dawn chorus as they travel across the country with the increasing light. The direction the birds take changes with the seasons. At the equinoxes they move across Britain from the east, but this changes in June as they fly down from the northeast. This weekend twitchers all over Britain will rise before dawn to take part in the survey to record their results, details of the weather and their location.

AROUND THE WORLD

"Moscow Opts Out"

Plans were announced earlier this year for May 23rd to be a celebration of the 250th anniversary of the Academy of Sciences in Moscow, to which leading scientists would be invited. However, these plans were cancelled. Newspapers from 12 of the 15 republics, however, gave glowing accounts of jubilee sessions called by their local academies. It is thought Moscow was concerned that Western scientists might become involved with local dissidents, particularly Jewish scientists who have been denied permission to leave Russia.

Cannes Film Festival

Devoted to global competition in the world of film, Cannes, on the Cote D'Azur is the annual focus for all things cinema. Started in 1946, for 2 weeks each May, this small but perfectly formed town on the French Riviera, is the venue for one of the world's major industries. The official competition with the top award - the Palme d'Or, has not only become a symbol of excellence but a reflection of the changes in the movie industry and continues to inspire new talent.

Previously, in 1938, the International Film Festival was the Mostra in Venice, and that year an American film was the unanimous favourite, but under pressure from Hitler, the Nazi propaganda film 'Olympia' won the Mussolini Cup. Furious, the other countries left Venice determined to hold an alternative festival the following year. A French film festival in Cannes on September 1st, 1939, was advertised. 2,000 invitations were dispatched to all film-producing countries including Germany and Italy, and a transatlantic liner rented by MGM docked in the Bay of Cannes. However, with the announcement of the German-Soviet Pact many tourists fled, and on the 1st of September, Germany invaded Poland and the only film shown that year at a private screening, was 'The Hunchback of Notre-Dame' starring Charles Laughton and Maureen O'Hara. Among other films never screened that year were 'The Wizard of Oz', and Britain's entry 'The Four Feathers'.

This week one critic wrote "The films must have been better in those old days... In the old days we saw no more than a couple of dozen in the course of the whole event, so it may be not so much that there are no good movies anymore; just that it's much harder to find the needles in a bigger haystack."

67

June 4th - 10th 1974

IN THE NEWS

Tuesday 4 — **"Hunger Striker Dies"** An IRA man died in Parkhurst jail on the Isle of Wight after being on hunger strike for more than two months. He was demanding to be treated as a political prisoner. Another IRA man called off his hunger strike after 200 days.

Wednesday 5 — **"Special Security"** Special Branch detectives in top hats and morning suits joined the 300,000 Derby crowd to guard the Queen against a possible IRA attack. Revenge raids have been threatened since the death of the prisoner on hunger strike.

Thursday 6 — **"Less Milk and Veggies"** Considered to be the worst drought in 50 years, the dry weather is having a detrimental effect on the size and yield of all food crops. The shortage of grass is affecting milk production.

Friday 7 — **"Sea Quest"** British Petroleum has made another big oil strike in the North Sea, about 145 miles north-east of Aberdeen. The company said the Sea Quest, had *'encountered encouraging oil indications.'* The use of the word 'encouraging' is being widely interpreted in the industry as indicating the discovery of a large oil-bearing structure.

Saturday 8 — **"Dr Who"** Known to millions of viewers as 'The Dr' John Pertwee is leaving The Tardis this week and will be replaced by Tom Baker. Pertwee starred previously in 'The Navy Lark' and appeared in four Carry On films.

Sunday 9 — **"A Bounty for Older Mothers"** 500 women at a Tory conference heard that *'instead of devoting their best years to raising families, women should be occupied in industry, science or the arts'* and be given a payment if they had *not* had any children by age 25.

Monday 10 — **"Prince Henry, Duke of Gloucester Dies"** The Queen's last uncle and the only surviving child of King George V and Queen Mary, has died aged 74. The funeral will be at Windsor, followed by interment in the royal mausoleum at Frogmore.

HERE IN BRITAIN

"Female Invasion"

The all-male Naval and Military Club in Piccadilly known to military wits as the 'In and Out' because of the signs on its twin doors, has merged with the 'Cowdray Club' for professional women. Two rooms have been set aside for the ladies use but they must still come in and out by the 'Ladies' Entrance' in Half Moon Street. Some areas will remain exclusively 'men only' including the 'Smoking Room', several bars, and at one end of the main dining room, a space known for some long-forgotten reason as 'The Coffee Room.'

AROUND THE WORLD

"D-Day Remembered"

A former French Resistance fighter, now Master of the steamer 'Villandry' organised a pilgrimage for Americans this week to commemorate those who died in the D-Day landings, 30 years ago. A wreath of red roses and carnations was cast into the Channel at dawn from the stern of the French ship, two miles off Arromanches.

About 250 pilgrims later enjoyed drinks to the piped music of Sid Lawrence playing Glenn Miller and the exhortations of General Eisenhower *'to be of stout heart.'*

THE OXFORD CROWN

One of the half-dozen surviving specimens of the 'celebrated Oxford crown' of 1644 by Thomas Rawlins was sold this week for £20,000. It is the most famous of the coins minted by Charles I at Oxford, when he set up his headquarters there at the start of the Civil War. The coin was worth 5 shillings at the time.

Despite his charm, Charles was out of touch with his subjects - at loggerheads with parliament over his military and domestic spending, and with the Protestant people over his tolerance of Catholicism. He repeatedly dissolved parliament when they refused him money, and eventually dismissed it altogether, resorting to raising funds through taxation. Faced with insurrections from the Scots and Irish, he recalled parliament to ask for money, but again met fierce opposition, and in 1642 Civil War broke out in England. Oxford, being both wealthy and relatively central, became the home of the royal court, in Christ Church, with counter-parliamentary sessions held in the Great Hall.

The Royal Mint was relocated to New Inn Hall Street, Oxford, also in 1642 and there, silver plate and foreign coins were melted down and, in some cases, just hammered into shape to produce coins quickly. The Oxford crown was minted in 1644 and shows the king on horseback, holding a sword in one hand and an olive branch in the other. Behind him is a view of Oxford with Magdalen College Tower in the forefront, the spires of All Saints Church, the University Church of St Mary, and the roof and tower of the Bodleian Library. The reverse details Charles's manifesto for his reign after the war – RELIG PROT: to uphold the Protestant religion, LEG ANG: the laws of England and LIBER PARL: the freedom of Parliament.

June 11th - 17th 1974

IN THE NEWS

Tuesday 11   **"Luck of the Irish"** An Irishman broke into a social security office and stole allowance books worth £750,000. But he never knew he had a fortune, as he dumped most of the books on a demolition site and made only £40 on the books he sold.

Wednesday 12   **"Lobster Gift"** A sea angler caught a 3lb lobster with a rod and line off the coast near Great Yarmouth. He has donated his catch to the nurses at Norwich Hospital, where he is an out-patient.

Thursday 13   **"Cheers for the Prince"** The Prince of Wales gave his maiden speech in the Lords and called for better coordination of leisure facilities to meet the challenge of *'removing the dead hand of boredom and frustration from mankind.'*

Friday 14   **"Red Arrows Behind Time"** The RAF's Red Arrows aerobatic team is to start a season of 30 displays on August 1, three months later than usual. Because of the oil crisis, training is four months behind schedule.

Saturday 15   **"A Fishy Tale"** A Bristol man caught a two-foot carp in the street outside his home after a lake in a park near by overflowed during a thunderstorm. Fish from the lake swam in the flooded streets as council workmen pumped away the water.

Sunday 16   **"TV Programmes Off"** 100 production assistants walked out of BBC studios at midnight on Saturday, halting the production of four programmes including an episode of a new Ronnie Barker comedy called 'Porridge'.

Monday 17   **"IRA Bomb in Westminster"** A 20lb gelignite bomb exploded at the Houses of Parliament. Eleven people were injured by the blast and a gas main fractured in the explosion and started fierce fires.

HERE IN BRITAIN

"What's in a Name"

The progress towards bilingual road signs in Wales, agreed by the government, will not be made without argument, a lost temper or two, and a sprouting of committees. There are bound to be revolts among pedants.

However, bilingual signing will not involve most of the place names of Wales, at least three-fifths of towns and villages have only one name, a Welsh one. However, the transition offers local authorities an excellent opportunity to tidy up place names and road signs which, even in English alone, are often badly sited, too abundant and confusing.

AROUND THE WORLD

"Princess Weds"

King Carl Gustav's youngest sister, Princess Christina of Sweden married her childhood sweetheart, businessman Tord Magnussan this week in the chapel of Stockholm Palace. The ceremony, which lasted an hour, was performed by the head of the Lutheran Church in Sweden in front of over 600 invited guests and was also televised for the nation.

The princess, who is 30, and the last of the 28-year-old King's four sisters to marry, says she *'intends to have one child and will keep up her nine-to-five job'*! The Princess is chairman of the Swedish Red Cross.

DESERT ISLAND DISCS

THE GENTLE MAN WHO TALKED TO 1,791 CASTAWAYS

FORTIETH ANNIVERSARIES: Roy and Paul McCartney

CAT CHAT: Roy with Princess Michael

DESERT ISLAND ROY

A hallmark of the BBC's weekly radio programmes, Desert Island Discs, the brainchild of producer and 'wannabee' actor, Roy Plomley, is now 52 years old. The first guest was marooned in January 1942, the edition having been pre-recorded in the iconic Maida Vale Studios which were the hub of the BBC's wartime news coverage during the war. Although at the time of the recording the building had been badly bombed, as with the rest of London *'it was business as usual'*. The first guest celebrity was the entertainer Vic Oliver, the music hall star, who also happened to be Winston Churchill's son in law.

The beauty of the programme was its simple format. Guests had to imagine being shipwrecked on a desert island and were asked which eight gramophone records they would choose to have with them. The gentle questioning by Plomley allowed for sometimes revealing interviews, but these early programmes were scripted, to comply with wartime censorship.

From September 1951, guests could choose a luxury item to take. Actress Sally Ann Howes chose garlic – food was still rationed at the time – and later that year, they could also choose one book to take together with the Bible and the complete works of Shakespeare which were assumed to be already on the island. The opening music remains to this day, 'By the Sleepy Lagoon' by Eric Coates, which was inspired by Bognor Regis - but is now a tune which will always be associated with the programme. Some listeners pointed out the seagulls, whose cries accompany the music, are herring gulls which would not have been heard on a tropical island and in 1964 they were replaced with tropical bird song. Following an immediate outcry by listeners, the gulls were returned!

June 18th - 24th 1974

IN THE NEWS

Tuesday 18 — *"Royal Ascot"* Despite the heavy security, including helicopters and patrols by dog handlers, the warm weather pushed any threat of violence into the background when the Queen drove down the mile-long straight at the head of a procession of open Landaus drawn by Windsor Greys, a tradition initiated by George, IV 149 years ago.

Wednesday 19 — *"Public Inquiry"* The Home Secretary will make a statement on the incidents in Red Lion Square, London, when police prevented a clash between a National Front demonstration and a counter demonstration by Liberation. One man died and 50 arrests were made.

Thursday 20 — *"Rocket Record"* Perth, Australia will witness the first solar eclipse in 50 years. Two rockets, travelling at 10 times the speed of sound will photograph the rare event 198 miles above the Earth.

Friday 21 — *"M3 Extension"* Despite protests that it will bring a *"tidal wave of traffic"* and traffic chaos to west London, the 12 mile extension of the M3, from Bagshot to Sunbury Cross, will open in July.

Saturday 22 — *"Gallantry Award"* The Queen has approved the creation of a new 'Gallantry Medal', which will rank in importance between the George Cross and the Queen's Commendation for Brave Conduct.

Sunday 23 — *"Sweet Taste"* Cough sweets bought by a woman in a shop in Buckinghamshire have been found to contain four times the permitted amount of arsenic. Four parts of arsenic in a million; the permitted content is one part a million.

Monday 24 — *"Secret H Bomb"* Harold Wilson revealed that Britain had secretly tested a nuclear device a few weeks ago, underground in America's Nevada Desert.

HERE IN BRITAIN
"The Big Squeeze"

Even fully allowing for a 'substantial shift' of freight and passenger traffic to rail transport, a continuing national roads programme is still necessary in Britain. However new roads in the future will be built to a lower standard to save money and land.

'We are not going to make roads worse; we are going to build on a less ambitious standard' was the comment from the Minister for Transport speaking at a press briefing. Some three lane roads would become two lanes and some dual carriageways will be reduced to two-way traffic.

AROUND THE WORLD
"Boisterous Scots"

15,000 Scottish fans who have travelled to watch their team play Brazil in the World Cup, have already upset the orderly burghers of Frankfurt with their boisterous behaviour. Many of them, dressed in tartan from head to toe, invaded an area of beer halls and sex shops in the city.

Kilted fans upset customers as they jumped on tables and smacked the bottoms of infuriated waitresses. In one beer hall the band leader railed *'You are not in Scotland now. This is orderly Germany. Behave, gentlemen.'* Trouble may be brewing for the police....

THE ORDER OF THE GARTER

Lord Shackleton, MP; Lord Trevelyan, Diplomat and Lord Abergavenny, Lord Lieutenant of East Sussex, were invested this week as Knights Companion of the Order of the Garter at Windsor Castle. The Order is dedicated to Saint George, patron saint of England and appointments are typically made in recognition of national contribution, or service to the Crown. Membership of the order is limited to the sovereign, the heir to the throne and no more than 24 living members, or Companions.

It is a chivalric order founded by King Edward III, who was fascinated with the legends of King Arthur, in 1348. After defeating the French at the Battle of Crecy he founded a College of St George at Windsor – a community of priests and 24 knights, each provided with a stall in the chapel. Women were originally associated with the Order in the Middle Ages, but this was discontinued until 1901, when Queen Alexandra became the first Lady of the Order of the Garter for over 400 years. The Sovereign can exclude members who have taken up arms against the Crown. In 1942, because of their hostilities during World War II, Emperor Hirohito of Japan was struck off the list of Garter knights and the Japanese imperial banner was removed from St George's Chapel.

Appointments are announced on 23rd April, which is St George's Day, and Garter Day takes place in June. After the Investiture ceremony, lunch is served in the Waterloo Chamber and then the procession makes its way to St George's Chapel for a service, accompanied by the Heralds and the Yeomen of the Guard all wearing full ceremonial robes and uniform. The public crowd into the streets of Windsor to see this historic spectacle, one of the major events in the 'royal watcher's' calendar each year.

JUNE 25TH - JULY 1ST 1974

IN THE NEWS

Tuesday 25 — **"First Drink at Home"** To combat growing alcoholism among teens, the National Council on Alcoholism recommends that young people learn to appreciate the use of alcohol under the influence of their home.

Wednesday 26 — **"Broadmoor Drug Trial"** Volunteers at Broadmoor are trialling a new drug to curb abnormal male sexual drives and deviations. No sexual offences were committed while the patients were receiving this treatment, nor for 3 years after the treatment ended.

Thursday 27 — **"Burtons Divorce"** Elizabeth Taylor and Richard Burtons' 10-year marriage was officially ended in a Swiss court, due to 'irreconcilable differences'. It was Taylor's 5th marriage and Burton's 2nd.

Friday 28 — **"French Voting Age"** The French National Assembly has decided to lower the voting age to 18 citing, *'It is high time to modify the rules of a society of the 19th century, which is largely obsolete'*.

Saturday 29 — **"Rabies Alert"** The British Veterinary Association has said that airport controls for handling and preventing the smuggling of animals that might be carrying rabies, ranged from 'thoroughly inadequate to practically non-existent.'

Sunday 30 — **"NZ says 'No' to Brits"** The New Zealand Immigration Minister told the parliament in Wellington *'The policy to restrict British immigrants since April is working and is working very effectively.'* Numbers have fallen sharply.

Monday 1 — **"Mr Pastry Returns"** Mr Richard Hearn is to don his 'Mr Pastry' outfit of bowler hat, cut-away suit, white tie, sloppy moustache and glasses, when the BBC series returns. 'Mr Pastry' originated in the 1936 stage show *Big Boy*.

HERE IN BRITAIN

"The Irish Sea"

An Antrim magistrate heard a case involving four men who were charged by the Northern Ireland Fisheries Board with failing to remove their salmon nets from the sea at the correct time and ruled that the waters around Ulster belong to the Irish Republic. Under the Government of Ireland Act, 1920, the Northern Parliament had powers relating only to the six counties of Ulster, the boundaries of which ended at the high-water mark. It could not therefore legislate for sea fisheries. Nine astute businessmen have already filed an application for prospecting in Ulster waters.

AROUND THE WORLD

"Salyut 3"

The Soviet Union has launched another orbital research station named Salyut 3. Links may be planned with manned space flights to coincide with President Nixon's visit this week.

The first Salyut, launched in 1971, was joined by the three cosmonauts from Soyuz 11 who died during re-entry because of a faulty valve in their spaceship. Western trackers said that a second Salyut, which broke up after tumbling out of control, was launched last year. Nine American astronauts are in Moscow to train with their Russian counterparts for a joint space flight next summer.

COVENT GARDEN CLOSES

It was announced that in November this year, the famous fruit, vegetable and flower market at Covent Garden in London will move after over 750 years to its new home south of the Thames to Nine Elms. It is one of four large wholesale markets in central London, together with the meat market at Smithfield, fish at Billingsgate and Leadenhall Market which sold poultry, game and other foodstuffs.

The present Covent Garden 40-acre site, with its kitchen gardens and orchard, once belonged to the convent of St Peter's, Westminster, and was known as 'the garden of the abbey and convent'. The Abbey was given by Henry VIII to the Earl of Bedford in 1552, and he developed the area with a large square surrounded by fine houses designed by Inigo Jones, to attract wealthy tenants. Jones designed the Italianate arcaded square and the church of St Paul's. The design of the square was new to London and had a significant influence on modern town planning, acting as the prototype for new estates as London grew.

By 1700 there was a regular market on the south side of the square selling produce, flowers and herbs from permanent stalls. Gradually, however, both the market and the surrounding area fell into disrepute, as taverns, theatres and coffee houses opened up and by the 18th century it had become notorious for its abundance of brothels. The Theatre Royal Drury Lane and Royal Opera House are close by, and the players would eat at Rules on Maiden Lane, the oldest restaurant in London.

The neo-classical building was erected in 1830 to cover and help organise the market and further buildings were added: the Floral Hall, Charter Market, and in 1904 the Jubilee Market.

JULY 2ND - 8TH 1974

IN THE NEWS

Tuesday 2 — **"New WRNS Commandant"** Princess Anne is to be the new Chief Commandant of the Women's Royal Naval Service. This position was held previously by Princess Marina for 28 years until her death in 1968.

Wednesday 3 — **"Fall of a Favourite"** Five times women's champion and 11 times semi-finalist, Billie Jean King of America, has been knocked out of the quarter finals of the Women's Singles at Wimbledon, losing to Russian, Olga Morozova.

Thursday 4 — **"School's Out"** Loss of strength in high-alumina concrete is being blamed for the closure of parts of at least 20 schools amid fears of structural collapse.

Friday 5 — **"Sweet Increase"** Steep increases in the cost of milk production will mean that chocolate will cost more. Shopkeepers are recommended to charge 1p extra for a 41p Dairy Milk bar and 14p more for a 68p box of Milk Tray.

Saturday 6 — **"Freedom of Speech"** The National Union of School Students voted overwhelmingly against preventing right-wing speakers from addressing schools. About a hundred delegates aged from 14 to 18, who represent more than 12,000 schoolchildren, rejected a motion to blacklist 'fascist and racist organisations.'

Sunday 7 — **"Refugee Airlift Completed"** Funded by donations from 27 different countries, nearly 250,000 people have been repatriated between Bangladesh and Pakistan. This should further the progress between the two Governments.

Monday 8 — **"Private Party - Public Money"** High winds and rain kept attendance at the weekend pop festival at Buxton, Derbyshire, below 20,000, however, the county will have to pay £30,000 for police work connected with the event, even though it was held privately.

HERE IN BRITAIN

"Hands Off Our Silver"

The Government is to stop the export from Britain of silver coins to other ECC countries for melting down because half-crowns and shillings (minted before 1947) can be purchased at below their silver value.

The Royal Mint's silver recovery programme has melted down half-crowns with a total *face* value of £86m producing silver worth £300m. £7m of coins worth £25m is thought to be still in the hands of banks and private individuals. It is an offence for an *individual* to melt down or break up coins.

AROUND THE WORLD

"Mail Treasure"

In Italy, mountains of undelivered mail was part of 400 tons of "wastepaper" which had accumulated in the chaos of a badly organised Post Office and sent to pulp factories for £6 a ton to be turned into cheap cardboard suitcases.

Carabinieri began investigating after a Post Office inspector found workers taking money and valuables from the envelopes. Cheques, postal orders and pension books were being picked out of the sacks. The Postal Minister said the *'chaos' was an invention of the press.'*

WIMBLEDON CHAMPIONSHIP

American Christine Evert won the 1964 Ladies Singles. Jimmy Connors won the Men's Singles

This week at Wimbledon, 19 year old Christine Evert of America won her first Wimbledon Ladies Singles title and Ken Rosewall of Australia reached his fourth final but was beaten by Jimmy Connors, also of America.

The first Championships were organised by the All England Croquet and Lawn Tennis Club in 1877 and was for men only. Twenty-two players entered, providing their own racquets and shoes whilst the club's gardener provided the tennis balls with their hand-sewn flannel outer casings. As lawn tennis was a popular sport, interest in the championships grew, and by 1884, when women were finally allowed to compete, regularly drew crowds numbering 3,000. By 1900, doubles and mixed doubles matches were also a regular part of the programme, as were players from overseas, but Britain dominated the winners until 1905 when an American claimed the Women's Singles title.

Although not classed as a regular Olympic sport, it did feature in 1908 when London hosted the games and the first televised Wimbledon broadcast was made in June 1937 with the programme limited to 30 minutes. During the first world war, the championships were held as usual, but many players didn't compete either because they took active roles in combat or were prisoners of war. Two German players, being members of Kaiser Wilhelm's personal staff, were held in British prison camps for the duration of the war. However, during WW2, for six years from 1940, no tennis was played at Wimbledon. In October 1940 a bomb hit the Centre Court causing extensive damage to the stands, meaning when the Championship re-opened in 1946, fewer spectators could be accommodated. Wimbledon is the most sought-after title in tennis because it's "the granddaddy of them all."

July 9th - 15th 1974

IN THE NEWS

Tuesday 9 — **"Power of Voodoo"** A self-styled high priest of the British Occult Society invoked the power of voodoo to put a death spell on two detectives. Clay dolls were sent to them with pins through the mouth and heart.

Wednesday 10 — **"Look Left, Look Right"** Children cannot remember the 1971 Green Cross code. *"Find a safe place to cross, then stop; stand on a pavement near the kerb; look and listen for the: traffic; if traffic is coming let it pass; look all round again; when there is no traffic near walk straight across the road, looking and listening for traffic while you cross."*

Thursday 11 — **"Rolls Royce Rarity"** An auction of vintage cars at Beaulieu in Hampshire, is to include a 1906 Rolls Royce which was used as a truck on an Australian tomato farm, and later found abandoned in the bush.

Friday 12 — **"Shankly Retires"** After 40 years in football and 14 years as Liverpool's manager, Bill Shankly has retired at the age of 59.

Saturday 13 — **"Glenn Miller Clue"** The wreck of an aircraft on the seabed off Dymchurch, Kent is to be investigated. It is sited near the spot where Glenn Miller, the bandleader, is believed to have crashed in 1944.

Sunday 14 — **"Last Parade"** About 300 of the remaining 1,200 elderly 'Old Contemptibles', members of the British Expeditionary Force which went to France in 1914, marched up Whitehall to Trafalgar Square.

Monday 15 — **"Half-Price Beef"** About five million old age pensioners and those on supplementary benefits would be eligible for cheap fresh beef under a plan put forward by the EEC Community's agricultural commissioner.

HERE IN BRITAIN

"£14 a Week"

The cost of running an average family car has risen by 27% over the past 12 months, meaning that it costs £746 a year to run a car between 1,000 and 1,500 cc compared with £578 this time last year.

This is the steepest increase on record. The main reason is the soaring price of petrol, with 'four star' now costing 60p a gallon (14p/litre), compared to 36p last year.

With a 16% increase in the cost of insurance premiums and higher parts and servicing costs, the age of cheap motoring has ended.

AROUND THE WORLD

"The Show Can Go On"

Frank Sinatra's concert tour is to continue as scheduled following a conference between trade union leaders and the singer's agents. A joint statement said that Mr Sinatra had not intended to make any reflections upon the moral character of Australian women reporters when he referred to them as 'hookers', but that he had meant only those who 'prostituted' their trade. Earlier Mr Sinatra offered to give three televised concerts in Sydney to be broadcast without charge. He also expressed regret *'for any physical injury sustained as a result of attempts to ensure his personal safety.'*

THE ROYAL BODYGUARD

The Queen inspected her Yeomen of the Guard this week with a parade, lunch and the usual photo call at Buckingham Palace. The royal bodyguard are known as 'Beefeaters' from the old custom of the crown paying part of their salary in chunks of beef! They were the original minders, forming a physical shield around the sovereign, ordering the royal meals, and even preparing the royal bed by stabbing the straw mattress with a dagger, searching for anything that should not be there.

Candidates today must have served in the armed forces for at least 22 years, attained at least the rank of Sergeant or Petty Officer, and been awarded the Long Service and Good Conduct Medal. Aged between 42 and 55, they can retire at 70. Whilst their duties no longer include stabbing the royal mattress each night, or ordering the royal take-away, they are in attendance at all major functions and ceremonials like the Maundy Thursday Service; the Epiphany Service at St James's Palace; all investitures and summer Garden Parties at Buckingham Palace; the installation of Knights of the Garter in St George's Chapel, Windsor; and at the coronations, lying-in-state, and funeral of the Sovereign.

One of their most famous duties is to perform a ceremonial search of the cellars of the Palace of Westminster prior to the State Opening of Parliament which remembers the Gunpowder Plot of 1605, when Guy Fawkes attempted to blow up both King James 1st and his Parliament. Yeomen still wear the red and gold Tudor uniforms with knee breeches, Tudor bonnets and ruffs, and a red cross belt, or baldric, worn from the left shoulder. They should not be confused with the Yeoman Warders of the Tower who are also known as 'Beefeaters' but whose dress uniform has no cross belt.

JULY 16TH - 22ND 1974

IN THE NEWS

Tuesday 16 — **"Bishops Removed"** Nine Greek Orthodox metropolitans (Bishops) were dethroned today, four as being 'uncanonicle' and five others were deposed as known 'troublemakers' who have strongly criticised the present Greek regime. The measures were taken to 'restore order to the Orthodox Church'.

Wednesday 17 — **"IRA Bomb Blast"** An IRA bomb placed in the Mortar Room of the Tower of London, exploded killing one person and seriously injuring 41 others. The Tower stonework in the Mortar Room also sustained some structural damage. Police say the bomb was detonated by a simple clock and battery mechanism.

Thursday 18 — **"Forced Feeding Stopped"** After months of controversy over hunger strikes by members of the Provisional IRA in British prisons, the Home Secretary has stated that the practice of forced feeding would be stopped. This is to deter hunger strikers.

Friday 19 — **"Stadium Safety Bill"** The Government has introduced a bill to safeguard sports spectators, by legislating that those sports arenas and stadiums with a capacity for more than 10,000 spectators should obtain a safety certificate from the local authority.

Saturday 20 — **"General Franco Hands Over"** General Franco has provisionally turned over his powers to his nominated successor, Prince Juan Carlos of Spain. This was shortly after doctors had announced that the General's health had worsened further.

Sunday 21 — **"Wrong Numbers"** Production of telephone directories has been delayed by at least three months due to an industrial dispute at Her Majesty's Stationery Office.

Monday 22 — **"Rubens Restoration"** The painting 'The Adoration of the Magi' by Rubens, which was scratched with the letters IRA in King's College Chapel, Cambridge, is being restored at no charge. Experts who offered their services have asked to remain anonymous.

HERE IN BRITAIN

"Plastic Food"

A high percentage of town waste is non-degradable plastic, which not only does not rot away but is also difficult to incinerate. However according to a report, this plastic could be turned into food for people and livestock. A team at Manchester University are looking at ways to turn waste plastic, which is rich in hydrocarbons, into proteins by an oxidation process using nitric acid. The oxidized products could then be used as food for micro-organisms like fungi which in turn can be used in human and animal food production.

AROUND THE WORLD

"Peking Protest"

Two workers from the Peking Arts and Crafts factory have complained that the heroic modern themes which were introduced during the Cultural Revolution, are being abandoned by the management, as statuettes of fat bellied Buddhas and famous concubines have been replacing revolutionary heroes in the workshops.

They are also prevented from displaying posters saying, *'We are the Chinese working class. We should have self-confidence and not be afraid of foreigners reading our posters.'*

BRASS BAND PROMS

Brass bands will be featured for the first time in this year's BBC Promenade Concerts which began this week. There have now been Promenade Concerts – literally, concerts where you can walk about, in London, for more than a hundred years and our present series can reasonably trace its ancestry to the entertainments in the public gardens of Vauxhall, Ranelagh and Marylebone in the eighteenth century.

The original English promenade concerts at the Lyceum Theatre in 1838 were conducted by Musard and consisted of instrumental music of a light character, containing overtures, solos for a wind instrument and dance music (quadrilles and waltzes). The change from theatre to concert hall, Queen's Hall, was made by Robert Newman when, in 1895, he started the present series with Henry J Wood as conductor. Newman wished to generate a wider audience for concert hall music by offering low ticket prices and an informal atmosphere, where eating, drinking and smoking were allowed. He said, *"I am going to run nightly concerts and train the public by easy stages. Popular at first, gradually raising the standard until I have created a public for classical and modern music."*

In 1927, the BBC saw that taking the concerts on would provide a full season for broadcast and would fulfil the Corporation's remit to 'inform, educate and entertain'. After the Queen's Hall was bombed in 1941 the Promenade Concerts moved to the Albert Hall where their policy remains, classics plus new works and among the established artists, promising newcomers. This season's newcomers, two leading Yorkshire bands, the Black Dyke Mills and the Grimethorpe Colliery, will be playing Elgar's 'Severn Suite', the 'Grimethorpe Aria' by Birtwistle, 'A Moorside Suite' by Holst, and Grainger's 'I'm 17 come Sunday'.

July 23rd – 29th 1974
IN THE NEWS

Tuesday 23 — "**Loan from Iran**" Iran is to lend Britain $1,200 million, for use on British public sector bodies. It will be made available as three separate yearly loans over the next three years.

Wednesday 24 — "**Child Minders Experiment**" Unregistered child-minders in Yorkshire are to be paid £10 a week from the Social Science Research Council grants, as part of a project to improve the care they offer children.

Thursday 25 — "**Pirate Radios Doomed**" The Dutch authorities are to ban three pirate radio stations broadcasting from vessels anchored off Holland - Radio Veronica, Radio North Sea International and Radio Atlantis.

Friday 26 — "**Britain's Fishing Rights**" The International Court of Justice in The Hague has ruled that Iceland cannot prevent British trawlers from fishing in their unilaterally declared 50 mile zone.

Saturday 27 — "**Smoking May Help**" Doctors at two London hospitals have noticed that smokers seem less likely than non-smokers to develop leg thromboses immediately after a heart attack.

Sunday 28 — "**Juggernautical**" Heavy seas and a high wind forced five young men from Northamptonshire to abandon their attempt to cross the Channel by bicycle to raise money for charity . They set off on a homemade raft of oil drums powered by four bicycles turning a paddle wheel, but had to give up two hours later, only five miles out.

Monday 29 — "**Lakes Flooded – By Visitors**" By October a new stretch of motorway and dual carriageway springing off the M6 will be capable of bringing 20 million people not only within day-trip range of the lakes, but at a steady 70 mph, to within seven miles of the eastern shore of Windermere.

HERE IN BRITAIN
"Primeval Wood"

A piece of the primeval forest of Britain, which has not been open to the public since the Middle Ages, was opened for one day only. It is in the 50-acre Groton Wood, in Suffolk, recently bought by the Suffolk Trust for Nature Conservation.

This ancient woodland is noted for its small-leaved lime coppice, indicating that the northern part of the wood has existed since prehistoric times. There are also large wild cherry trees and 22 seasonal ponds. There is abundant wildlife, including great-crested newts, woodcocks, and 15 species of butterfly.

AROUND THE WORLD
"The Man Who Will Be King"

Prince Juan Carlos became Acting Head of State in Madrid this week. He is a cultured, 36-year-old sportsman, fluent in several languages. Educated in Spain under the watchful eye of Spain's dictator, General Franco, Juan Carlos has been groomed for the throne from early days.

He now has provisional powers covering the absence or illness of the chief of state, which he will hold until the event of the death of the critically ill General, at which time he will automatically be named King. The prince is married to Princess Sophia with three children.

GOLDSMITHS COMPANY

The leopard's face in the Goldsmiths Company crest is used as their hallmark.

THE GUILDS AND LIVERY COMPANIES OF THE CITY OF LONDON

Prince Richard of Gloucester has been admitted into the freedom of the Goldsmiths' Company with modest ceremony and lunch with the court of assistants at Goldsmiths' Hall. The Worshipful Company of Goldsmiths has been one of the Twelve Great Livery Companies of the City of London since 1327. Items made in precious metals were required to be of a set standard and over the next 150 years various marks were introduced which identified the maker, the year of manufacture, and the place or Assay Office where it was hallmarked.

The company is also actively involved in ensuring the accuracy of all coins produced by the Royal Mint by means of 'The Trial of the Pyx.' This is one of the oldest judicial procedures in the country dating back to the 12th century. The name Pyx, from the Latin word for box, refers to chests in which the coins are transported. For centuries they were stored in the Pyx Chamber in Westminster Abbey, along with other important items of state and church.

The first recorded trial was in 1248 when twelve citizens and twelve goldsmiths of London were selected to examine the money. The Trial is a formal court of law held annually at Goldsmiths' Hall to check that UK coins produced at The Royal Mint are within the statutory limits for metallic composition, weight and size, and it is presided over by the Queen's Remembrancer, a senior judge of the Royal Courts of Justice. Still unchanged since mediaeval times, throughout the year, coins are randomly selected from every batch of each denomination struck, sealed in bags containing 50 coins each, and locked away in the Pyx boxes for testing when the Trial takes place. The Company has two months to test the coins.

JULY 30TH – AUG 5TH 1974

IN THE NEWS

Tuesday 30 — **"Bi-lingual Charter"** A Tory MP has asked the Privy Council to review its decision and allow the charter for the borough council for his constituency of Llandudno and Conway be in both Welsh and English.

Wednesday 31 — **"Italian Travel"** Visiting motorists from Britain will now be allowed coupons for 400 litres (87 gallons) of cheap petrol. The coupons can be collected at Italian tourist offices throughout the country.

Thurs 1 Aug — **"Bards Prepare for Battle"** Attendance at the Eisteddfod has increased in recent years and tickets for next week's event in Carmarthen are already difficult to come by.

Friday 2 — **"Film Rejected"** 'More about Language of Love' has been refused a certificate by the British Board of Film Censors, who said it contained sequences like the film 'Deep Throat' although the reviewers said, *'It was a serious sex-educational film, in no way titillating'*.

Saturday 3 — **"Minimum Wage"** The TGWU, Britain's largest union, which until recently had been calling for a £25 a week minimum wage, has now upped the figure to £30 a week target and is calling for support to wipe out *'the scandal of low wages'*.

Sunday 4 — **"Coppers Brew Up"** As part of a campaign to emphasize the dangers of driving while tired, Devon police have been serving tea to drivers in a lay-by on the A38 holiday route.

Monday 5 — **"Low Pressure"** The promised sunny Bank Holiday weekend weather did not materialise. The south had torrential rain and storms, but the New Forest B & B's reported record trade from campers who were forced to abandon their tents.

HERE IN BRITAIN

"Cardiff Rations"

A Cardiff supermarket has restricted customers to one 2lb bag of sugar because of a national shortage. *"We are trying to protect regular customers from people who go swanning from shop to shop buying nothing but sugar!"*

Cadbury Schweppes makers of Corona soft drinks have also cut their output, not just because of the sugar shortage but also because of shortages of bottles and jars. If it gets any worse, there won't be bottles to put drinks in. The company has raised the deposit for standard bottles to 4p, almost half the price of the drink inside.

AROUND THE WORLD

"Go-ahead For Greek Tours"

Following the Cyprus settlement between the Greek and Turkish governments, a cautious green light is now being given to holidaymakers still planning to go to Greece. Many flights have been scheduled over the weekend, with tour operators planning to resume their activities in Greece and the islands immediately.

However, the Foreign Office has warned that any deterioration in the Cyprus situation could lead to Greece reimposing some travel restrictions at short notice but say that currently travel agents can offer holidays and business travel services to Greece.

OPEN AIR THEATRE

The Regent's Park Open Air Theatre season is in full swing and boasts several superlatives when it comes to 'all things drama'. It is the oldest, professional, permanent outdoor theatre in Britain, and has one of the largest arenas in London, which is itself the 'Theatre Capital' of the United Kingdom, with over 200 theatres in the city.

The 18-week season attracts up to 140,000 playgoers each year and has been a favourite venue for over 40 years. It was opened in 1932, and in the years leading up to the war, put on a whole variety of productions, starring the great stage names of the day. In 1939, there were only matinee performances as blackout restrictions were in force, but along with the Windmill Theatre, it could brag that 'it never closed!' Then in 1945 it was back to business as usual with a full schedule of performances. Comedies dominated the post-war programmes as people tried to put the war behind them. The actors too had something to celebrate when in 1949, brick dressing rooms were built to replace the draughty, damp tents they had used previously. The mid 1950's saw the start of many overseas engagements, as the company took the Open Air Theatre first to Lebanon, and then to over 20 different countries in subsequent years, including Russia, Egypt, Israel and Dubai.

This year has seen a massive £150,000 upgrade to the amphitheatre, including fixed seating, and will also be followed by a new box office, kitchen and picnic lawn. Both traditional and modern plays feature in each year's programme, and many have been written specifically for the theatre. However, one of the most popular productions to feature regularly is Shakespeare's 'A Midsummer Night's Dream', a perfect choice for an outdoor summer evening.

AUG 6TH - 12TH 1974

IN THE NEWS

Tuesday 6   **"Reject Tyres"** A dealer was fined £1,950 for selling reject car tyres. The British Rubber Association had warned last April that such tyres imported from Germany and Italy, were intended for use only on low-speed agricultural vehicles.

Wednesday 7   **"People Are Leaving Britain's Big Cities"** The recently published 1971 census confirms that people are living longer and relocating out of the large cities..

Thursday 8   **"Royal Streaker"** A nude man ran across the deck of his yacht in front of Princess Alexandra and the Duke of Edinburgh at Cowes. He was about to dive off his boat and had no idea royalty was only 15 yards away. He later apologised saying he *'had no swimming trunks on board and wanted to keep his jeans dry.'*

Friday 9   **"Nixon Resigns"** *'This was a serious act of omission for which I take full responsibility and which I deeply regret.'* Nixon resigned after admitting that he had withheld information at the Watergate hearing and Gerald Ford took the oath of office 30 minutes later.

Saturday 10   **"Robinson College Cambridge"** The new University college will be named after the former head of Robinson TV Rentals, who donated £10m towards building costs.

Sunday 11   **"Drugs Bust"** More than two and a half tons of cannabis, worth just over £3m, the biggest quantity of illegal drugs ever discovered in Britain, are being held at Liverpool in two crates addressed to the United Arab Emirates Embassy in London.

Monday 12   **"President in Exile"** The exiled President of Cyprus, Archbishop Makarios, received an enthusiastic welcome from the Greek Cypriots community in London yesterday when he celebrated Mass at an Orthodox Church.

HERE IN BRITAIN

"Drama at The Proms"

Patrick McCarthy was a staunch 'Prommer', as well as a student at the Guildford School of Music & Drama. On 7th August he had been rehearsing his first professional operatic role, before heading to The Albert Hall to hear Thomas Allen, also a baritone, singing from 'Carmina Burana', a cantata Patrick knew well. However, at the end of the 2nd solo, Allen collapsed and had to be taken off the stage. Unfortunately, the understudy was the doctor looking after Allen, so Patrick stepped into the breach in a borrowed dinner jacket and saved the performance.

AROUND THE WORLD

"Les Halles Site To Be Turned Into a Park"

Ever since the central Paris fresh food market was levelled by bulldozers last year, there has been controversy around the future of its Les Halles site, which has housed a market in one iteration or another since the 11th century. Under President Pompidou the site was to house an international commercial centre with modern office buildings, the foundations of which had been started some time ago, but work has been suspended since last June following his death. President Giscard d'Estaing has decided against the planned commercial centre, favouring landscaped open spaces instead.

TRAINING SHIP FOR SALE

The training ship 'Arethusa', moored on the Medway at Rochester. Lord Shaftesbury (inset).

The training ship 'Arethusa', moored on the Medway at Rochester, has been a training and boarding school for boys for the past 40 years, but is now up for sale.

In the 19th century, Lord Shaftesbury, a philanthropist and campaigner for the rights of children, had the idea of providing refuge to destitute young boys in London, and promoted the idea of naval training ships to set them up for a career in the navy. He persuaded the Admiralty to loan a 50-gun redundant frigate, the 'Chichester' which was fitted up and moored on the Thames at Greenhithe. Its first intake was 50 boys from a children's refuge in Covent Garden. An early task was teaching the boys how to swim, although there were several instances of them falling overboard and drowning. Of the original 50 who had joined, records show 21 joined the Merchant Navy, 9 joined the Royal Navy, 7 returned ashore, 1 was apprenticed to a tailor, 2 drowned and 1 died of fever. Training included compass work, splicing and reefing sails, steering the ship, maintaining the ships log, knots, signals, as well as cooking, cleaning, tailoring and carpentry. The original Chief Officer's wife was awarded £20 per year for teaching the boys how to cut out and make their own clothes from material supplied by the Navy.

In 1873, a second training ship was established, the 'Arethusa', a wooden frigate which was the last to have gone into battle under sail. However, her condition deteriorated and in 1932, her replacement was found, the present 'Arethusa', a steel-hulled barque, built in Hamburg in 1911, on which the boy's training continued until recently. The sale is being held under the rules of the Charity Commissioners and the ship will go to the highest bidder.

AUG 13TH - 19TH 1974

IN THE NEWS

Tuesday 13 — "Right to Strike" Equity, the actors' union, voted for a clause forfeiting the right, made in an agreement more than 35 years ago in exchange for a closed shop, for artists working in the West End, to be removed immediately from all contracts.

Wednesday 14 — "Cycle Hire" A collaboration between the Countryside Commission and the British Cycling Bureau means visitors to the National Trust's Clumber Park in Nottingham will be able to hire bicycles to explore the 3,000 acre property.

Thursday 15 — "Wallies Move 10 Yards" The authorities served eviction notices on the 'Wallies', a commune of young people, once 50 of them but now only eight, who have been camped at Stonehenge since the Summer Solstice on June 21st. Wally Keith said, *"We don't want any hassle, man. Let the light of love and peace shine through."*

Friday 16 — "Holiday Makers Stranded" The government are backing a rescue operation of 40,000 stranded holidaymakers after the collapse of Clarksons & Horizon Holidays. The prospects for 150,000 people with confirmed bookings are uncertain.

Saturday 17 — "Russian Dam" Authorities have approved plans to build a 16-mile flood-breaking dam across the Finnish Gulf to protect the low-lying city of Leningrad.

Sunday 18 — "Stranded on Big Dipper" Three holidaymakers were stranded 60ft up for 20 minutes before being rescued by firemen at Battersea Funfair. An official said, *"The people did not seem a bit bothered, but they did not come back for a second ride."*

Monday 19 — "Alligator Stolen" A 2ft alligator was stolen from its tank at the Horniman Museum in London. A museum spokesman said, *'It needs to be kept in tepid water'.*

HERE IN BRITAIN

"Lime And Sewage"

Organisers of the three-day free pop festival in Windsor Great Park planned for the August bank holiday are expecting over 100,000 young people.

However, Windsor and Maidenhead council are worried by the prospect, and are considering spreading lime or sludge from Slough sewage works on the site to keep the thousands of young people away.

The council secretary said, *'The festival is totally illegal, and we mean to take steps to keep the number of hippies to a minimum... last year Windsor became a hippy colony for over a week.'*

AROUND THE WORLD

"Olé for Women"

In another blow against male chauvinism, legislation has been passed which allows women to compete in bull fighting, opening up thousands of bull rings in Spain to women matadors, and ending a three-year fight by Senorita Angela Hernandez, who has fought bulls for the last seven years in South America, for the right to fight alongside men.

Until now the 27-year-old has been barred from fighting bulls in Spain, but with the support of many other Spanish bull fighters, including El Cordobes the celebrity matador, she took her case to court.

WORLDLY ESPERANTO

ESPERANTO

ADJECTIVES

alta	=	tall
bela	=	beautiful
facila	=	easy
granda	=	big
longa	=	long
nova	=	new
pura	=	clean
sana	=	healthy
seka	=	dry
varma	=	warm

All adjectives in Esperanto end with A.

LEARN ESPERANTO

amiko	=	friend
arbo	=	tree
birdo	=	bird
domo	=	house
hundo	=	dog
kato	=	cat
libro	=	book
strato	=	street
urbo	=	city
viro	=	man
amikoj	=	friends
arboj	=	trees
birdoj	=	birds
domoj	=	houses
hundoj	=	dogs
katoj	=	cats
libroj	=	books
stratoj	=	streets
urboj	=	cities
viroj	=	men

A British-born Professor of English Literature who teaches in Philadelphia, has been elected President of the World Esperanto Federation at the age of 35. Although Esperanto is not a major world language, it has quite a following today, particularly in Europe and parts of the Far East. It was the idea of a Polish doctor in the 1880's to have a common language that could bring the global community closer together.

Although Dr Zamenhof's dream of world peace never materialised, the language lives on. Based on European languages, it is easy to learn and pronounce. Although a medical doctor, Zamenhof was no amateur at languages, speaking nine fluently and having a working knowledge of three of the classical languages, Latin, Hebrew and Aramaic, from school days! Many devotees abandoned Esperanto with the onset of World War I, seeing the ideal of world peace disintegrating, and later in World War II, it was banned by Hitler, who wrote in Mein Kampf that it was *'a language being used by Jews as a method of world domination.'* However, with the end of the war there was a slow resurgence of interest, as travel and trade were opened up again, and international agencies such as NATO and UNESCO were formed and the United Nations became more prominent on the world stage.

There is an annual congress known as the Universala Kongresso, which this week was held in London. Not only is the language used in international business circles, but many books and plays have been translated into Esperanto. Among famous people who speak it fluently are the author J.R.R.Tolkien, Harold Wilson the PM, and William Shatner, from the television series 'Star Trek', who learnt it specially for his part in the film 'Incubus'.

AUG 20TH - 26TH 1974

IN THE NEWS

Tuesday 20 — **"IRA Break Out"** 19 leading members of the Provisionals broke out of Ireland's top security prison at Portlaoise, blasting down the doors of the jail with high explosives. Two of the most important IRA officers in the country were among those who got away.

Wednesday 21 — **"Hunt for Escaped Wolf"** A wolf is being hunted in Black Park, Slough, after it escaped from Pinewood Studios, where the film 'Legend of the Werewolf' is being made.

Thursday 22 — **"Hawks First Flight"** A new British jet fighter-trainer aircraft, the Hawker Siddeley Hawk, made its first successful flight from the company's airfield at Dunsfold, Surrey.

Friday 23 — **"Victims Champions"** On this date Richard III supporters place notices in the "In Memoriam" column of The New York Times. This year there were also notices from 'Plantagenet', supporters of the Princes in the Tower and others killed by the King.

Saturday 24 — **"800 Yard Leap"** Stunt man, Evel Knievel, will attempt a jump across the sheer sided Snake River Canyon, Idaho, on a rocket-powered motorcycle. If successful, he will win $6m, but if not, $6m insurance will be paid to his widow.

Sunday 25 — **"Britain's Tipple"** Inhabitants of the British Isles still have the world's greatest thirst for sherry, according to figures from Jerez. Great Britain and Northern Ireland bought 722,293 hectolitres last year, nearly 60% of the total exported.

Monday 26 — **"Scott's Cross"** A 10ft wooden cross which commemorates Captain Scott on Observation Hill, above McMurdo Base, was blown down in an Antarctic storm. Scott died on the return journey after reaching the South Pole in 1912.

HERE IN BRITAIN

"Turbary, Piscary and Estovers"

A Hampshire man invoked the medieval rights of turbary, piscary and estovers over the gardens of some of the people in his village which would give him rights to 'dig up people's gardens, take goldfish from their ponds and graze horses on their property.'

However, it was found at a court in Winchester that the land is not held in common and the 'proceedings were a farce, wilfully false and biased and were without foundation.' Detectives are investigating allegations by some firms that they had paid money to release building land from his claim.

AROUND THE WORLD

"Jungle Survival Training"

A German ship's officer smuggled a year-old orangutan out of Borneo and then tried to sell him to European zoos. He was persuaded to hand the ape over to The World Wildlife Fund rather than be prosecuted for trafficking an endangered species.

Now the orangutan has been returned to Borneo from West Germany to be trained at a rehabilitation centre in the art of jungle survival. Game department officials hope that this example of world-spanning concern will help to stamp out the illegal sale of young orangutans, which are normally captured by shooting the mother.

BARTLEMAS DAY

St Bart's Hospital in London (left) and St Bartholomew's Hospital in Sandwich (below) which is the centre of giving Bart's Buns to children on Bartlemas Day.

Saint Bartholomew was supposedly martyred by being flayed alive and this connection has made him the patron saint to butchers and tanners and by extension to bookbinders, for one of their traditional materials for binding books is leather. The Saint is best associated with two institutions, St Bart's Hospital in London and the ancient St Bartholomew's Fair. However, the Cinque Port of Sandwich in Kent also celebrates St Bartholomew's Day each August 24th. Among the most cherished institutions of the town is their St. Bartholomew's Hospital, not a traditional place for the sick, but a tranquil setting for the aged men and women of the town.

About 50 years ago the old hospital building of the Middle Ages was replaced by a quadrangle of little cottages, each standing in its garden with the ancient chapel in the centre. Each year children run round the chapel and receive a current bun from the trustees of the hospital. The adults are presented with a less edible 'St Bart's biscuit', a wafer stamped with the town's coat of arms. But despite these meagre offerings, it is a day for foodies. As he was the patron saint of butchers, roast beef and pork are traditionally on offer washed down with copious amounts of ale. But for the sweet toothed and youngsters there are apples dipped in honey – the forerunners of our toffee-apples.

Honey, in its alcoholic form is celebrated in Gulval, Cornwall, where on this day there is the Blessing of the Mead ceremony, with much sampling. The beef served on this day is traditionally called Bartlemas Beef, which according to a recipe of 1664 is a piece of brisket marinated for 3 days in wine, vinegar and spices, made into a brawn and eaten with mustard and sugar.

AUG 27TH - SEPT 2ND 1974

IN THE NEWS

Tuesday 27 — **"Charles Lindbergh Dead"** Charles Lindbergh, the American who in 1927 became the first man to fly solo across the Atlantic, has died in Hawaii aged 72.

Wednesday 28 — **"Whirlwind Descends on Garden"** A whirlwind ripped off a shed roof and uprooted a 70ft willow in Surrey. The roof landed on the summer house where the owner and his wife were having breakfast. The Met Office say it was probably a small tornado.

Thursday 29 — **"Bumper Harvest"** The most valuable grain harvest in Britain's history, about £850m, is being gathered. It is expected to reach a total of 15 million tons.

Friday 30 — **"Film Musical Banned in Santiago"** The film 'Fiddler on the Roof', has been banned in Chile. A spokesman said it contained *'disruptive elements against Chilean harmony and the process of reconstruction'*.

Saturday 31 — **"Never Lost for Words"** Dr John Sykes has won the 'Cutty Sark Times National Crossword Championship' for a third successive year. He is a lexicographer, and the editor of the Concise Oxford Dictionary, which, he admits, might give him a marginal advantage over his rivals.

Sun 1 Sept — **"Rally in Hyde Park"** A rally in Hyde Park to support demands for a public inquiry into police brutality at the Windsor Free Festival last week, passed without incident. MP's have called for a permanent pop festival site.

Monday 2 — **"Jewel of Venice Saved"** After 26 months' restoration work by experts from the V & A Museum in London, funded by the 'Venice in Peril Fund', the Loggetta at the base of the campanile in St. Mark's Square was handed back to the Mayor of Venice.

HERE IN BRITAIN

"Change for Harris Tweed"

An overhaul for the Harris tweed industry has been proposed by the people who weave, market and promote the famous cloth. They want a change in the law that rigidly determines how the tweed should be made, regarding the 'Orb Trademark', granted in 1909, as an archaic law.

One stipulation is that the tweed must be produced by hand on a single-width loom. The Highland board are advocating a power driven, double-width loom, to enable them to produce cloth 54 inches wide and placate the 'disgruntled and dwindling work force' and modernise the industry.

AROUND THE WORLD

"Picasso's Gift"

The Spanish painter Pablo Picasso had expressed the wish that his private collection should go to the French people following his death in April last year.

Now, in accordance with that wish, 41 paintings by some of the greatest names in the art world are housed in their final home at The Louvre in Paris, where they will be hung in one large single room, as stipulated by the artist.

The collection includes pieces by classical artists; Chardin, Le Nain, and Corot as well as works by his contemporaries; Rousseau, Matisse, Renoir and Cezanne.

BRITISH FORCES NETWORK

An outside broadcast to troops (main) with presenters and performers Harry Secombe, Cliff Michelmore and Roy Castle (insets).

General Eisenhower's '7th Principle of War' was all about raising troop morale, and the British found that the best way to do this, apart from having 'Monty hand out cigarettes', was to open a radio station. Using BBC personnel, they did just that in 1943. The British Forces Network, now BFBS, is known for keeping calm under fire and recent evidence in Cyprus has shown just that. The broadcasters who manage the 6 stations on bases around the world call themselves 'The Professionals', and are on air for 14 hours every day, with a schedule of thirds. One third of items are locally originated, another is in the form of tapes from London, featuring the Top 20 hits, sport, features and home news. The final third contains items from the BBC World Service.

Best known of the BFBS centres is undoubtedly Cologne, where Cliff Michelmore launched his career with 'Two Way Family Favourites'. Every Sunday at midday in this country, countless Sunday lunches were prepared to the sound of the theme music, 'With A Song in My Heart'. It was also where incidentally, Cliff found his wife, Jean Metcalfe, who was the London presenter of the same programme. They did not actually meet for six months, but Michelmore called their romance *'Love at first hearing'*.

As was shown in Cyprus, the stations not only entertain, but also put out essential announcements, direct evacuees, and generally make themselves useful, sometimes staying on the air 24 hours a day while any crisis is ongoing. Not everything is straightforward broadcasting, however. The BBC organise live entertainment on a combined services basis, with stars such as Harry Secombe, and Roy Castle as compères, and they are always able to attract big names to special events.

Sept 3rd - 9th 1974

IN THE NEWS

Tuesday 3 — **"Football Parasites"** Prison sentences, bans on attending matches, and fines were imposed by magistrates on violent football supporters in various parts of Britain.

Wednesday 4 — **"Teacher Shortage"** A call for 100,000 ancillary helpers to ease the burden of teachers was made by the National Association of School Masters. They envisage a pool of women who would be paid perhaps half to two-thirds of the teachers' scale-one salary.

Thursday 5 — **"BBC 2 Poachers"** BBC 2 is to compete for viewers against BBC 1. BBC 1's popular nine o'clock news programme will go up against a series of comedy and light entertainment programmes, including Call My Bluff, and two series of Monty Python and M.A.S.H.

Friday 6 — **"Poster Protest"** Tories protested to the Labour Party Chairman about the poster that appeared in Rome on the first day of the European Athletics Championships. The poster read *'Britain will win with Labour'* and was picked up by BBC and ITV cameras.

Saturday 7 — **"Scorpion in Laundry"** Health officials in Reading are concerned by the discovery of a deadly yellow European scorpion in a local laundry, as they fear that others may be at large in the town.

Sunday 8 — **"The Pandas Are Coming"** Two pandas presented to Britain during Mr Heath's visit to China last May, will soon be leaving for London. A British Airways aircraft will fly from Hong Kong to pick them up.

Monday 9 — **"Full Pardon for Nixon"** Richard Nixon was granted a full pardon yesterday by President Ford for all the offences which he may have committed while in office.

HERE IN BRITAIN

"Morning Cloud"

Gale-force winds and torrential rain caused widespread flooding on the South coast and forced shipping to seek shelter this week. Mr Heath's yacht 'Morning Cloud' was wrecked off Jersey after dragging its anchor, and yachts were torn from their moorings at Falmouth.
Coastguards reported the busiest day of the year for Essex and Kent lifeboats and a rescue helicopter from Manston, Kent, was also dispatched.
In Sussex there was damage to beach huts, and boats were drawn up on the shore, when the roughest seas of the summer broke 20 feet high above promenades.

AROUND THE WORLD

"Italian Pop Fraud"

Italian pop singers and the heads of 12 record companies are under investigation in connection with a huge fraud during the 1972 edition of the popular television song contest and lottery Canzonissima.
The fraud was discovered after Italy's Finance Ministry, which runs the lottery, discovered that one-third of the 18 million slips used by the public to vote for the winner and take part in the lottery, were forged.
Experts painstakingly peeled the slips off a sample of 600,000 cards and, as it was impossible to detect the forgeries, each was tested chemically.

THE STONE OF SCONE

STONE OF SCONE
A replica of the stone upon which the Kings of Scots were crowned on Moot Hill until 1296 when Edward I took the stone to Westminster Abbey.

A replica of the Stone of Scone can be seen in the grounds of Scone Palace, Scotland.

A tiny electronic device under the seat of the Coronation Chair functioned so efficiently that it put a hundred police officers at Scotland Yard on high alert and foiled a plan to steal the Stone of Scone from beneath it.

Some people suggest that the stone was Jacob's Pillow, brought from the Holy Land, eventually arriving at Scone in the 9th century to be used in the crowning of Scottish kings. When the King of Scots rebelled against England in 1296, Edward I marched north and removed what he believed to be the Stone to Westminster. There, it was mounted beneath the seat of a wooden throne, so when an English king was seated there, he was also, symbolically, the ruler of Scotland.

On Christmas Day in 1950, a group of four Scottish students broke into Westminster Abbey and removed it, but as they took it from the Abbey the Stone broke in two. They drove the larger part to Kent and buried it in a field until the nationwide hue and cry - which included the first closure of the border between Scotland and England for more than 400 years - had died down. Then they took both parts to Glasgow where a stonemason made the necessary repairs. Finally, in April 1951, they left the Stone at Arbroath Abbey and tipped off the police, who returned it to Westminster Abbey. But despite the return of this potent symbol of Scottish nationality, the question remains: is the stone in Westminster the real one? Or did the monks fool Edward, by handing over a copy all those centuries ago? If so, the Stone on which successive kings and queens, including the present monarch, Elizabeth II, have been crowned since the 14th century, is nothing but a lump of rock.

Sept 10th-16th 1974

IN THE NEWS

Tuesday 10   **"Three Golds"** On the last day of the European Athletics Championships in Rome, Brendan Foster won gold in the 5,000 metres, Ian Thompson in the marathon and the 400 metres relay team.

Wednesday 11   **"Khrushchev's Only Monument"** The former Russian Prime Minister lies in an ordinary Moscow cemetery, his monument an abstract bronze bust of which he once said, *'A donkey with his tail could do better.'*

Thursday 12   **"Scottish Tourism"** Edinburgh gains from tourism but also suffers from thousands of visitors each day. One local said, *'They break fences, trample everywhere. The villages overflow and so do the septic tanks.'*

Friday 13   **"Maze Prison Protests"** Belfast was sealed off by dozens of hijacked buses, cars, lorries and taxis when both loyalists and republicans set up barricades in protest at the ban on food parcels at the Maze prison at Long Kesh.

Saturday 14   **"£10 per Week for the Disabled"** As an alternative to the invalid tricycle, disabled people are to have £4-a-week mobility allowance whether they can drive or not. Plus, those who have never been able to work will have a £6-a-week pension.

Sunday 15   **"Parachute Drop"** Sir James Stuart-Menteth, a legless former Scots Guards officer, plus three other disabled ex-Servicemen, parachuted into the Solent from 2,500ft to promote the British Limbless Ex-Servicemen's Association.

Monday 16   **"Brian Clough Dismissed"** Brian Clough, manager of Leeds United for seven weeks, was sacked last night, after a dressing room meeting the players reported a vote of 'no confidence'.

HERE IN BRITAIN

"Sociologist Witch Doctor"

A professor of sociology at Stirling University, presented a paper on witchcraft, telling the meeting that he, *'takes every opportunity of claiming my status as a witch doctor and this sometimes means people have curious expectations of me. However, I don't propose to indulge in any 'smelling-out' ceremonies or to transform this occasion into an orgy.'* He added he'd once attended a grave-watching ceremony to prevent sorcerers exhuming and consuming a corpse, *'Because something special'* had been painted on his forehead he was invisible to witches.

AROUND THE WORLD

"Emperor Haile Selassie Dethroned"

Haile Selassie of Ethiopia, who had reigned for 44 years, was dethroned this week. Army tanks surrounded the palace at 5am.
Members of the Armed Forces Coordinating Committee went to the 82-year-old Emperor and read out to him the proclamation deposing him, repeating their accusations of his corruption and neglect, and establishing a provisional military government. In keeping with the new regime's more modest style he was transported in a Volkswagen car, accompanied by a heavily armed escort.

Unlucky For Some!

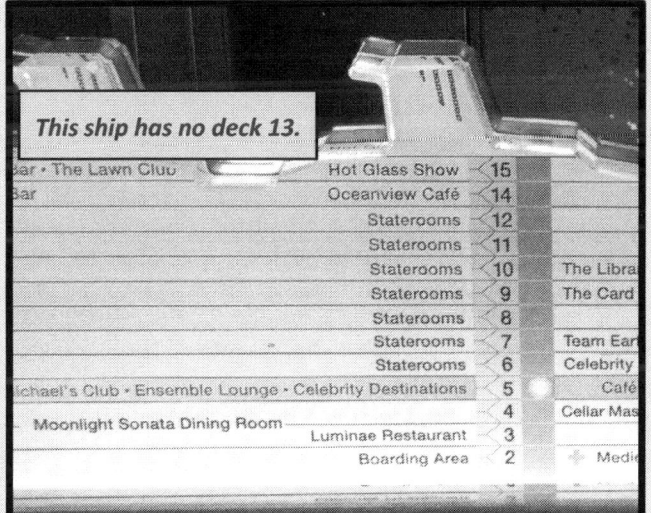

This ship has no deck 13.

XIII DEATH

LA MORT

When a man appeared before the magistrate faced with a charge of abduction, in that, *"he did steal and unlawfully carry away"* Police Constable Charles Wright, he might well have wondered about the day and the date. It was Friday 13th. For many, Friday 13th which occurs one to three times per year is regarded as a most unlucky day. Superstitions surrounding the date are thought to originate in the middle-ages and there are dozens of fears, myths and old wives' tales associated with the date all over the world. Some people even suffer from Triskaidekaphobia, the fear or avoidance of the number 13 or 'Paraskevidekatriaphobia', the crippling fear of Friday the 13th.

The number 13 and Friday both have an individual long history of bringing bad luck. In the Bible, Judas, who betrayed Jesus, was the 13th guest to sit down to the Last Supper. In Norse mythology, a dinner party of the gods was ruined by the 13th guest called Loki, 'god of deceit and evil', who caused the world to be plunged into darkness. Peoples of the Mediterranean, regarded 13 with suspicion, not being as perfect as 12, which is divisible in many ways.

As for 'Friday', according to tradition, Adam and Eve were expelled from Eden; Cain murdered Abel; St John the Baptist was beheaded the enactment of the order of Herod for the massacre of the innocents, all took place on a Friday. In Chaucer's Canterbury Tales, written in the 14th Century, he says 'and on a Friday fell all this mischance'. Here in Britain, Friday was once known as 'Hangman's Day' because it was usually when people who had been condemned to death would be hanged and the great crash of 1869, when the price of gold plummeted, was on Friday too.

SEPT 17TH - 23RD 1974

IN THE NEWS

Tuesday 17   **"Chinese Pandas"** The giant pandas Ching-Ching and Chia-Chia met the British public for the first time at London Zoo. They arrived on a non-stop flight from Peking where they travelled in a specially equipped cargo jet, with bamboo shoots, oxygen masks, and ice blocks to sit on if they got too hot.

Wednesday 18   **"Meals Ban Ends"** Catering staff at six Liverpool hospitals have ended a 48-hour ban on serving meals, after a hunger strike-by 15 protesting patients at Liverpool Royal Infirmary.

Thursday 19   **"Food for Pandas Ching-Ching and Chia-Chia"** Bamboo shoots from a convalescent home in Hampshire are helping to feed London Zoo's two giant pandas. They munch their way through 500lb of shoots a week.

Friday 20   **"Secret Moves"** Plans to deter motorists from taking their cars into central London by charging them up to £1 a day were revealed in a confidential document leaked to several national newspapers.

Saturday 21   **"Mercury Images"** Photographs of the south polar region of Mercury relayed by Mariner 10, complete a survey of nearly 40% of the planet.

Sunday 22   **"Development Threat"** A colony of artists' and craftsmen's studios and shops at Camden Lock, in north London, is threatened by a proposed development of offices, flats, shops and a pub, which, they say, will change the character of the area.

Monday 23   **"Beer is Best"** A report from the Merseyside Council on Alcoholism shows that beer is still the most popular alcoholic beverage for British drinkers, despite entry into the EEC and consumption of more things European.

HERE IN BRITAIN

"CEEFAX"

Ceefax, the first teletext service in the world went live on 23 September. It was a 'spin off' from work the BBC were doing to provide televisual subtitles for deaf people and began with 30 pages of information.

Designed to transmit a page of text during the nightly "close-down" period of transmission, to see a page of required text, the user would enter a three-digit page number and the selected page would display on the screen. Before the Internet became popular, Ceefax pages were often the first location to report a breaking story or headline.

AROUND THE WORLD

"Pariah Ship"

Japan's first nuclear powered ship has fallen foul of the Japanese's over whelming fear of radiation after Hiroshima and Nagasaki. For nearly two years, fishermen in the port of Mutsu blockaded the vessel to prevent it sailing on a test run to fire its reactor. She recently managed to escape during a typhoon but ten days later, instruments detected a radiation leak and with the reactor deactivated she headed back under diesel power. Now, fishermen have threatened to drop 30,000 bags of ballast into the port and over 1,000 small boats have blocked the harbour entrance again.

Punch and Judy

Mr Punch is 312 years old this year and, despite his disappearance from street corners, there is life and vigour in him yet, as it is estimated that there are about 70 or 80 Punch showmen in Britain today. Our favourite puppet character has had a varied career since he arrived in this country in 1662, brought by an Italian showman from Bologna. Originally called 'Pulcinella', he was a character of the Italian Commedia dell'Arte, a travelling theatre group who began to appear on puppet stages in the early 16th century. He was popular around Europe, but it was only in England that he remained a traditional figure. Initially he was not a wife-bashing, murderous villain, but more of a sharp-tongued comic clown, a bit lecherous; kissing, jumping on ladies' laps and making vulgar jokes about the politics and scandals of the day. It was most definitely an 'adults only' show in those times!

In the early 18th century, marionette shows were popular with everyone, and Punch even had a theatre in Covent Garden devoted to him, but by the end of the century the large company puppet shows had gone out of fashion and the showmen took to performing solo on the streets, using glove puppets in place of marionettes. It was at this time that the show took on the form we know today. Punch's wife changed her name from Joan to Judy in 1818 and a regular cast of up to 14 characters was assembled, including Dog Toby. There are various theories as to his origins but the most likely is that he was based on a real bulldog used by the showman to guard his flimsy stage from damage and theft while he was working the puppets.

Almost all remaining Punch and Judy shows are at sea side resorts, and have been a popular entertainment for children and adults alike.

Sept 24th – 30th 1974

IN THE NEWS

Tuesday 24   **"A Clean Sweep"** An honours graduate in chemical engineering, has left his teaching job to become a chimney sweep. He found he could match his teacher's wage of £1,900 a year in just 25 hours work with vacuum and brushes.

Wednesday 25   **"Better ITV Reception"** 625-line relay stations in Wales and Derbyshire, were opened by the Independent Broadcasting Authority. They will improve reception for 25,000 viewers.

Thursday 26   **"Canal Workers' Dispute"** Northern towns Blackburn, Burnley and Leeds face the threat of flooding because of a proposed strike by canal workers. The British Waterways Board was taking immediate action by lowering the pounds (dams) between locks.

Friday 27   **"Radioactive Waste Glass"** British Nuclear Fuels Ltd have published plans to convert liquid radioactive wastes, mixed with a slurry of glass-forming silica and borax, into solid glass which can be used in the construction industry.

Saturday 28   **"Money Free Fall"** A man threw handfuls of £10 notes from the back of a green, flat lorry on the main Barnsley to Wakefield road in Yorkshire. Motorists handed £1,030 to the police, who said, *'You have to admire their honesty.'*

Sunday 29   **"Troops at Heathrow"** The Army moved back into Heathrow airport with armed soldiers and police patrolling approach roads in anti terrorist stop-and-search car checks.

Monday 30   **"Bound for San Francisco"** A full-size replica of Drake's flagship, 'The Golden Hinde', left Millbay Dock, Plymouth, bound for America on its maiden voyage. It has been constructed to be the centrepiece for the 400th anniversary celebrations of Drake's supposed landing in San Francisco.

HERE IN BRITAIN
"Barnsley Bitter"

The MP for Barnsley addressed nearly 2,000 members of the Campaign for Real Ale who held a protest march through the town against the proposed closure of Barnsley Brewery.

Courage plan to close it by 1976 and move everything to their brewery in Tadcaster, resulting in the loss of 200 jobs in Barnsley and the disappearance of Barnsley Bitter, a famous local brew which has sustained generations of South Yorkshire miners.

In his speech he said, *'the big brewers were using their near monopolistic powers to steamroller through the indiscriminate closure of the smaller breweries.'*

AROUND THE WORLD
"Too Cool for Comfort"

The West Germans are becoming a nation of shoplifters, many of whom are male and 25% are schoolchildren. One woman filled her fur coat lining with stolen food whilst other women go to the supermarket with 'shoplifting bags' hidden under their skirts.

One unfortunate man took a fancy to a frozen chicken which he concealed under his hat, but he was detected at the cash desk when he fell unconscious while waiting to pay for other items. The frozen bird on top of his head had slowed down the blood circulation to his brain.

SHEPPERTON SALES

To mark the end of the re-organisation of the sprawling 20-acre site, Shepperton Studios will become a vast auction room at the end of this month. Surplus equipment, props and bric-a-brac used in many of the greatest British films made since the war, go under the hammer to make way for the new streamlined film-making centre, firmly geared to today's competitive market.

Staff mingled with auctioneers, press photographers and reporters, and sadly surveyed the neatly stacked, labelled and penned impedimenta of past glories: relics of 'Oliver', 'Colditz', 'Richard III', 'Guns of Navarone' and, appropriately, 'End of the Affair'. Wire pens were filled with enough umbrellas to stock a lost property office and there were boxes filled with cricket bats and skis, artificial flowers, mistletoe, mess tins from Colditz, number plates and dummy shells. In this land of fantasy, nothing is quite what it seems: gold bars turn out to be feather light, the champagne bottles are empty but surprisingly, the hundreds of books are real. There are male and female mannequins and models of sharks, aliens, airships and flying saucers. There is even a Bechstein grand piano and a magnificent oil-fired steam boiler, which an auctioneer insisted on describing as antique.

There has been a rush of orders for sale catalogues, and the viewing times have been extended for the benefit of the local people. The property supervisor described it as a sad time. *"What the fog, smoke, snow and bubble machines will fetch is anybody's guess. Most of the money will come from the sale of cameras and equipment."* But he was cheered by the fact that films that would not otherwise have been made in the old studio with its huge overheads, will be more than possible in the newly refurbished studios.

OCT 1ST - 7TH 1974

IN THE NEWS

Tuesday 1   "Canal Workers' Strike" The canal workers' strike severely disrupted Goole Docks, with 6 ships trapped and 14 ships queuing in the Humber Estuary. Canal water tops up the docks and this had to be conserved for industry.

Wednesday 2   "The High Life" At a trial at the Central Criminal Court, a witness said that prostitutes in the West End competed to see which one could keep her 'manager' in the highest style. Many paid £100 a week to members of a vice gang known as 'The Syndicate'.

Thursday 3   "British Design in Demand" A British theatre design exhibition has opened in Bordeaux. Among the designers whose work is exhibited are Sir Cecil Beaton and Jocelyn Herbert of the Royal Court Theatre.

Friday 4   "Militant Victory" Mineworkers' leaders rejected the National Coal Board productivity scheme linking higher pay to higher output. Moderates were humiliated when only four members voted against the Yorkshire militants.

Saturday 5   "Publican Saved Lives" IRA bombs exploded in Guildford pubs crowded with Army recruits. The Seven Stars' landlord heard the explosion at the nearby Horse and Groom, and safely evacuated his bar before a bomb also destroyed his pub. 5 were killed.

Sunday 6   "Tip Plan Protest" Countryside and literary enthusiasts joined forces objecting to Coal Board plans for a 120ft dirt tip, half a mile from Newstead Abbey, the home of Lord Byron.

Monday 7   "Queen's Award" A British Airways engineer has received the Queen's 'Commendation for Valuable Service in the Air.' He supervised the escape chutes for more than 100 people in the 'whisky hijacking' in Amsterdam early this year.

HERE IN BRITAIN

"Gin And Knickers Divorces"

'All you do is fill your wife with gin, give her a complacent lodger and file your petition. Or a husband could say he found it impossible to live with his wife because she wears pink knickers.' A judge said that *'connivance and collusion having gone under the new divorce laws, this was all that was necessary to get a divorce nowadays.'*

In the case before him he refused to grant a decree because the petitioner failed to use the vital, but 'idiotic' phrase, *'they found it intolerable to live with their marriage partner'*.

AROUND THE WORLD

"Portuguese 'Labour Day'"

This week on the celebration of the foundation of the republic of Portugal in 1910, the Prime Minister appealed for everyone to do a day's work on Sunday, for the nation.

The Roman Catholic Church dispensed its members from the day of rest for the occasion and trains ran weekday schedules taking commuters to work and those who could not get to their usual trade worked as volunteers cleaning up cities and towns. Students volunteered to rid Lisbon of the hundreds of thousands of tattered political posters and graffiti that deface the walls.

WELSH STRUGGLES

Once there was the curious tale of an inn which straddled a wet-dry border. On Sundays the public bar was dry and empty, but the lounge bar was wet and crowded.

As pub opening time approaches on Sundays, some men in Wales still walk, or even drive, across the county boundaries to get their Sunday pint. Or they belong to clubs. Or they may even go for a ride in the buffet car of the Ffestiniog railway, which is a thin, wet line in a Sunday-dry Gwynedd. *'It really is a ridiculous situation,'* said the hotelier chairman of the Seven Day Opening Council, *'Day visitors to Wales who walk into an hotel will see guests drinking at the bar, but they themselves, not being guests, cannot be served. We aim to remove this anachronism and make all of Wales wet on Sundays.'*

However, the secretary of The Temperance Committee of the Baptist Church Union of Wales, said, *'The figures for alcoholism and absenteeism are increasing. Wales would be better off if people drank less or gave it up. And as far as Sunday is concerned, we regard it as a special day and, as the last poll showed, people of five counties wanted to keep the old tradition.'* Therefore, in pulpit and public bar, in manse and hotel lounge, the battle plans are being drawn up. On one side, in the fastnesses of Welsh Wales, are the last defenders of that once mighty Welsh institution, the quiet family Sunday unstained by alcohol. On the other, and growing in strength, are licensees, the drinking classes and plain citizens who maintain that the Welshman's right to a Sunday pint, to say 'Iechyd da' (good health) to his friends in all parts of Wales, should no longer be denied.

OCT 8TH – 14TH 1974

IN THE NEWS

Tuesday 8 — **"Sugar Beet Harvest"** Few processing factories have enough supplies of sugar beet to continue working as heavy rain has prevented harvesting. Deliveries to industrial customers are at risk.

Wednesday 9 — **"Lost For 16 Years"** An umbrella lost in 1958 by a vicar from Highbury, whose name was engraved on the handle, has been found on a London bus and is being returned to him.

Thursday 10 — **"Narrow Victory for Labour"** Harold Wilson won the second General Election of the year putting Labour in power but with a smaller majority than expected.

Friday 11 — **"Before Their Very Eyes"** Prospectors who unearthed a huge frozen mammoth's tusk in the Russian oilfields of Tyumen watched helplessly as it turned from white to yellow on contact with warm air.

Saturday 12 — **"Military Clubs Bombed"** Two bombs exploded in the basement of the Victory Ex-Service Club in Seymour Street, Marylebone, and simultaneously, there was an explosion at the Army and Navy Club in St James's Square, just off Pall Mall.

Sunday 13 — **"Rising Crime Rate"** Juvenile crime is on the increase in West Yorkshire. Police are putting it down to the rise in the school leaving age. *'Some juveniles seem to get bored by being kept at school. If they were allowed to get jobs, they would have more to interest them.'*

Monday 14 — **"Submariners Saved"** Two American men were rescued after being trapped for more than six hours on the floor of the North Sea 170 miles east of Dundee in a midget submarine. The submarine was working on an oil rig anchor installation when a rope fouled its propeller.

HERE IN BRITAIN

"Coal to Replace Oil"

Over the next 20 years, oil will become too valuable to burn as fuel, a spokesman from the National Coal Board said in a discussion on progress into research into more effective ways of using coal as a direct energy source.

The most vital use of coal will be as *'a high-quality source of petroleum, light fuel oils and synthetic materials. The world is only just beginning to realise the true value of coal. It is a rich storehouse of reserves of energy and raw materials which we are beginning to unlock.'*

AROUND THE WORLD

"Operation Swallows"

The general public have been asked to help migrating swallows trapped by winter's sudden onset. Thousands of the birds have died of hunger because cold and high winds have killed off the insects on which they feed.

The appeal, 'Operation Swallows', asked people to shake bushes, or light fires under tree branches to drive out insects for the birds to feed on. People have also been asked to collect and feed exhausted birds. Swiss Railways and Swissair are carrying cardboard cartons of swallows free, for release on the other side of the Alps.

ENGLISH VINTAGES

English wine, still the laughingstock of the British public, is increasingly sought after by connoisseurs in the States, Australia, Canada and Japan. Ten years ago, no more than 1,500 bottles of English wine were produced and although a wet July may well halve the crop, we are still expecting to produce around 120,000 bottles this year. These wines, which are mostly a light, dry, white wine, are of medium to good quality, selling at £1.20 to £1.80 a bottle and there are now about 40 commercial vineyards in the country with 385 acres of vines in the South and East of England.

Almost anyone can grow vines. A great deal is said about the amount of sun, soil types and a south-facing slope. But there are only two really important things, good drainage and wind protection. A vine needs only 150 days of about 10°C during its growing season. It can grow on almost any type of soil, including chalk, as indeed all champagne vines are. But there is a great deal of difference between English wine, which is grown, fermented and bottled in this country, and British wine, which is made from an imported grape juice concentrate, and is mostly made into port or sherry rather than table wine. It is felt that much of the prejudice against English wine comes from its association with the relatively cheap, largely low-quality British wines.

The chairman of the English Vineyards Association, says, "*I do not think we shall ever produce a Château Latour, but we can produce a good wine. Our climate, awful though it is, is no problem. We can overcome most problems, but it is the acceptance by the public and by the trade that is the really dodgy issue.*"

OCT 15TH - 21TH 1974

IN THE NEWS

Tuesday 15   **"Fleet Air Arm Exhibition"** Princess Anne made an official visit to open the Fleet Air Arm Museum at the Royal Exchange, in the City of London.

Wednesday 16   **"Maze Prison Riots"** Provisional IRA and 'loyalist' prisoners set fire to huts and attacked prison officers at the Maze Prison internment camp at Long Kesh outside Belfast.

Thursday 17   **"Dad's Army"** Some of the TV show's cast visited the Home Guard exhibition at the Imperial War Museum. 'Corporal Jones' drove his butcher's van through the gates of the Museum, parked outside the magnificent portico and said to Admiral Sir Deric Holland-Martin, *'Nice house you've got.'*

Friday 18   **"Electric Cars"** Battery-driven buses, vans, cars and even trains are expected to be operating in Britain in large numbers within 10 years because of technical advances in the lightweight sodium-sulphur battery, making Britain a European, if not a world, leader in the field.

Saturday 19   **"Speed Saved Beaches"** After a three hour long crude oil spillage at Milford Haven, from the 250,000-toll tanker Texaco Great Britain, five spray-boats pumped detergent on the area straight away, and a later search showed no oil was left.

Sunday 20   **"Archbishop For TV"** The Archbishop of York, Dr Coggan, who will become Archbishop of Canterbury in December, is to appear regularly in a new series of 'Stars on Sunday', the ITV programme, starting in November.

Monday 21   **"Vatican Eases Ban"** The Vatican has partly eased its 200-year-old ban on Catholics joining the Freemasons. Catholics in countries where the society 'does not conspire against the church' will no longer be excommunicated.

HERE IN BRITAIN

"£11 an Inch"

The eight 'My Fair Lady' clinics in London and Manchester have closed because the group has gone out of business. Beneath the clinics' emblem of a svelte and sylph-like female posing on one toe upon a pink rose, overweight ladies, missing their appointments, were apprehensive about getting their money back.

The clinics specialised in heat treatments, massage and exercises to reduce too solid flesh and promote the thin woman struggling inside every fat one to get out. Courses cost several hundred pounds, which worked out at about £11 for every inch off the waistline.

AROUND THE WORLD

"Community Wine Glut"

According to a report from Brussels, wine sales in non-producing members of the EU is continuing to rise, with consumption in Britain and Denmark more than doubling over the past five years, but in producer countries like France, it remained virtually static, and Italy drank significantly less last year than 5 years ago.

The report confirms that last year's record-breaking wine harvest means that the Community has extremely large excess stocks, which are proving difficult to disperse due to increased imports from Cyprus, Bulgaria, Yugoslavia and Algeria.

TRAFALGAR DAY

Sunday 21st October
Trafalgar Day Lunch

Join us to commemorate Nelson's famous victory

Trafalgar Day is an annual celebration observed on October 21, commemorating the Royal Navy's victory over the French and Spanish at the Battle of Trafalgar in 1805. France was the dominant military force led by Napoleon, a great soldier. However, the Royal Navy ruled the seas and, in this battle, Nelson captured 18 French ships, forcing Admiral Villeneuve to surrender.

However, the Battle of Trafalgar is perhaps remembered most for the death of Admiral Horatio Nelson aboard HMS Victory. His body was placed in a cask of brandy mixed with camphor and myrrh, which was then lashed to the Victory's mainmast and placed under guard. At Gibraltar the body was transferred to a lead-lined coffin filled with spirits of wine. Arriving eventually at the Nore on the Thames, Nelson's body was placed inside a lead coffin which was encased in a wooden one made from the mast of his ship 'L'Orient' which had been salvaged after his greatest victory, the Battle of the Nile. After a four-hour service at St. Paul's Cathedral, he was finally interred within the crypt, in a black marble sarcophagus originally carved for Cardinal Wolsey.

Nelson's skill and bravery was such that he was claimed a national hero, with many monuments erected throughout Britain in the years following his death. On Trafalgar Day, his monuments are decorated with flags, banners or laurel swags, and wreath laying ceremonies are held during the day in his honour when the famous Trafalgar flag signal "England expects that every man will do his duty" is flown from Nelson's Column in London and on Carleton Hill, Edinburgh. In the evening, at specially held commemorative Trafalgar Night dinners, a speech is made which always ends with a toast to "The Immortal Memory of Lord Nelson, and those who fell with him".

Oct 22ND – 28TH 1974

IN THE NEWS

Tuesday 22   **"Chaos in Glasgow"** Three thousand bus and underground crews in Glasgow are on unofficial strike and six thousand road haulage drivers, also on strike, are seriously affecting Scottish industry.

Wednesday 23   **"Warning for Fireworks"** Following a prediction by the director of a fireworks reform campaign to have counter sales banned within a year, the Fireworks Makers' Guild have warned that the sale of dangerous black-market fireworks would rise.

Thursday 24   **"Child Allowance"** The Child Poverty Action Group is calling on the Chancellor to raise the family allowance to £3.20 for each child. At present, an allowance is only paid for the second child (90p) and £1 for all subsequent children.

Friday 25   **"To the Duchess, a Son"** The Duchess of Gloucester, formerly Miss Birgitte van Deurs of Denmark, gave birth to a son. The baby, ninth in line to the throne, will use the title of Earl of Ulster.

Saturday 26   **"Danger on Cornish Beaches"** Dangerous Russian made smoke floats containing explosive have washed up on Cornish beaches. Smoke floats are typically used in a marine accident for indicating a position.

Sunday 27   **"Savings Stamps"** The National Savings stamp, an introduction to saving since 1916, is to be phased out. Stamps are sold door to door, and the savings movement has 150,000 volunteer workers. It will be a blow to many people who *'rely on them to buy their TV licence or pay their bills'*.

Monday 28   **"The Sun Rise"** The rising cost of paper and production is blamed as the reason for the increase in price of The Sun daily newspaper by 1p, to 5p.

HERE IN BRITAIN

"Money To Burn"

Inland Revenue inspectors became interested in the family's poultry farming business when Mr Sharp 'with no more than £50 to his name', died without having declared a further £16,000.

His son, now a director of the Yorkshire company, also kept quiet about it, but when it became clear that the authorities were 'on to him', to 'protect his father', Sharp took the extraordinary step, giving a new meaning to the expression 'money to burn', burnt the cash and buried the ashes in a rose bed in the garden. The IR inspector dug up the rose bed!

AROUND THE WORLD

"Poison Water"

According to press reports, Italian neo-fascists have been planning a coup to take place this autumn, starting with the poisoning of Rome's water supply and the assassination of prominent officials. The Italian Defence Minister has confirmed that The Red Brigade, who are Italian, right-wing terrorists, had planned to poison Italy's domestic water supply with uranium. He told the defence committee of the Italian Chamber of Deputies that the terrorists had planned to steal radioactive material from a nuclear centre in Northern Italy and use it to poison a number of aqueducts.

PHILLIPS MOVE UPMARKET

Phillips, the London auctioneers, began with a big sale in Westminster in 1798, selling works imported from the art gallery of the guillotined Marie Antoinette and household items from Napoleon Bonaparte and Beau Brummel. This made Phillips highly popular among the aristocracy and was one of the most popular options for handling their sales, especially for auctioning off the contents of country estates. Harry Phillips the firm's founder mixed his business skills with his charming personality creating entertaining and elegant evening receptions before each sale and it remains the only auction house to have ever held a sale inside Buckingham Palace. During the first decades of the 20th century, the commodities auctioned at Phillips were of a great variety, ranging from houses to paintings, from lace work to wine, and from furniture to building materials. After a devastating fire in 1939 which totally destroyed its long-time headquarters, the auction house was forced to relocate to new premises across the street.

This week saw the celebration of the 20,000th sale in their Bond Street premises. They are the third largest fine art auctioneers in London and this important milestone in their history is being celebrated with a week of important auctions and the launching of an advertising campaign. In the past their secret to success has been in the rapid turnover of a large volume of middle-range antiques, £100 - £5,000, but now they are definitely moving up-market and as well as fine art, they sell fine walnut furniture, tapestries, good Chinese porcelain and very expensive jewellery. This requires more specialised expertise and Phillips have been gradually dividing out their departments into specialisations. There are no receptionists, only direct lines, so each department has a team of experts who answer the private, sometimes clandestine, inquiries.

Oct 29th – Nov 4th 1974

IN THE NEWS

Tuesday 29   **"Russia Launches Unmanned Luna Spacecraft"** Russia has launched another unmanned space craft, Luna 23, to 'continue exploration'. Luna 22 has been studying the Moon's cosmic radiation and magnetic fields.

Wednesday 30   **"HM as My Witness"** Two brothers accused of committing a nuisance in front of the Queen, by raising a banner calling for increased ex-Service pensions, have requested her Majesty to appear as a witness on their behalf. A court official said 'no chance'.

Thursday 31   **"Risks of the Oil Boom"** The Church is to make a study of the social and moral dangers connected to the development of North Sea oil which has brought an influx of money and increased drunkenness into remote areas.

Friday 1   **"Sugar Men Block Refinery"** Supplies of sugar are now almost unobtainable in most areas, because of the protest against the agreement to import increased quantities of refined European sugar in place of unrefined Commonwealth cane.

Saturday 2   **"No Perk"** At Norwich magistrate's court Norwich, the prosecution said, *'While a football match years ago used to be regarded as one of the 'perks of the job' by the police, it is now the reverse. Policemen are routinely spat on, threatened and assaulted.'*

Sunday 3   **"Opera House Approved"** The revised design for Edinburgh's opera house has been approved, although the Fine Art commission has asked the designers to reduce the height of the fly-tower, which is to house scenery at the top of the building.

Monday 4   **"New Uniform Scrapped"** British Airways' new summer uniform for stewardesses, designed by Hardy Amies, has been abandoned after cabin crew protested that it would make them look 'frumpish' and 'dowdy'.

HERE IN BRITAIN

"Dolls Secured"

The V & A have successfully purchased 'Lord and Lady Clapham', two rare, 'William and Mary style', 17th century dolls in period costume, and their elaborately carved wooden chairs, for £16,000. It is thought they belonged to descendants of the diarist Samuel Pepys. An agent for a Swiss collector bought the dolls at auction earlier this year, but the Board of Trade banned the valuable dolls' export. Now a consultant to experts on The Antiques Road Show, the agent has finally persuaded her client to allow the Museum to purchase them, assuring they would remain in England.

AROUND THE WORLD

"Baptising Wine"

The trial of 18 wine dealers has opened at the Gironde Assizes where they are charged with fraudulent dealings in Bordeaux wines. Inspectors uncovered a chain of dealers leading to some of the most respected names in the wine trade. The fraud involved mixing mediocre red wines with a little white to reduce the tannin levels and create a much better taste. One defendant explained, *'80% of the Appellation Controlee wines are wonderful quality. The rest are only very modest and need to be doctored before they are sold. It is common practice, and it is called baptism'.*

Scout and Spy

Ralph Reader

Ralph Reader, leader of the Scout Gang Shows, retired this week and it was revealed that he had worked for British Intelligence during the Second World War. He was recruited in 1936 to cultivate young RAF apprentices and former scouts using the Gang Shows as cover. Not aware that The Ministry of Intelligence were using his reports to track down fifth columnists and enemy agents, it wasn't until 1938 that he was informed of the importance of his role. He still has the 1942 Air Ministry letter marked 'secret', which confirmed him as an intelligence officer with access to the Director of Intelligence.

Under the guise of giving concert parties, Reader haunted bars looking out for German speakers and tracking down the origins of subversive literature that was reaching Servicemen. He had one coup, just before Dunkirk. *'I was sitting in the Lion d'Or when a fellow came in, left his hat with the hat-check girl, had one drink, recovered his hat and left.'* Thinking it suspicious, he reported it and was ordered to keep watch. The same thing happened three days later. Years after the war, reading a military history, he discovered the outcome. *'The girl was slipping into the man's hat information she had picked up from pilots using the bar. She was eventually shot.'*

When war was declared he went into the RAF and was sent off to France after instruction in counter-spying. That included cutting out the personal columns of newspapers and studying them for oddities that might be agents' messages. He looks back as cheerfully on his secret exploits as he does on the Gang Shows, those patriotic entertainments so deeply evocative of the 1940s, and so extraordinarily durable ever since. *'I loved it'*, he says. *'I had the time of my life.'*

Nov 5th - 11th 1974

IN THE NEWS

Tuesday 5 — **"Dream World"** Failed Asian undergraduates in Britain's white-collar workforce are not making plans to return home. Instead, they are sustaining a 'dream world', fearing their 'façade of success' would crumble, and expose the reality to their families.

Wednesday 6 — **"Prison Breakout"** Twenty prisoners escaped from The Maze prison and despite helicopter, police and army dog searches, two remain missing. They dug a 65-yard tunnel with spoons for their escape.

Thursday 7 — **"Lighter Relics of War"** An Imperial War Museum exhibition has opened with displays of manuscripts, letters, and belongings of six major poets of WW1. Rupert Brooke, Siegfried Sassoon, Wilfred Owen, Edmund Blunden, Isaac Rosenberg and Edward Thomas,

Friday 8 — **"Lord Lucan Disappears"** Scotland Yard are investigating the disappearance of Lord Lucan. He is wanted for questioning about the murder of his children's nanny and a vicious attack on his wife.

Saturday 9 — **"All Clear"** Forty lorries, from eight contractors, have been brought in to clear up the rubbish left out on the streets during a dustmen's strike in Chelsea and Kensington. The strike arose from the arrest of 30 dustmen charged with obtaining money by menaces.

Sunday 10 — **"Medieval Lid Missing"** A rare 13th century lid of a hanap, or medieval wine goblet, is missing from All Souls College in Oxford. It has been conservatively valued at £15,000.

Monday 11 — **"Dinner with The Goons"** The Prince of Wales joked with Spike Milligan, Peter Sellers and Michael Bentine, before a private dinner at the Dorchester to launch their book. The fourth Goon, Harry Secombe, was ill, but sent a poem called 'Ballad from a Sick Ned'.

HERE IN BRITAIN

"Three Minutes to Go"

31 sticks of gelignite packed into a shopping bag, was found by a porter at the rear of a building housing the Inland Revenue in Wolverhampton. One of the largest bombs used in the IRA's current urban bombing campaign in England.

The porter said, *"I opened the bag and saw a clock and batteries and knew immediately what it was"* He carried it 15 yards to put it between two concrete blocks to minimize the blast at about 10.57. The army report indicated the bomb had been due to go off at 11.00, but failed to detonate.

AROUND THE WORLD

"Dutch Prove To Be Sober Drivers"

Holland's first breathalyser tests show that the Dutch are remarkably sober when driving. Of 40,000 drivers, including motor cyclists, who were stopped during the night at the weekend, only 51 were found to be over the legal limit.

The police breathalysed 317 of the motorists and, although not liable to prosecution, only 92 had to hand in their car keys and walk home, but one policeman was killed by a driver who refused to stop. Under the new law, the level of alcohol per gram in a driver's blood must not exceed 0.5 milligrams.

REMEMBER REMEMBER

*'Remember, remember, the 5th of November, gunpowder, treason and plot,
I know of no reason why powder and treason, should ever be forgot!*

So runs the traditional rhyme which commemorates the failed attempt by thirteen Catholic activists to blow up the Protestant King James I and his parliament in 1605. The plotters were executed and shortly after, an Act of Parliament declared 5th of November a public holiday, with compulsory attendance at church to give thanks for the failure.

Although the act was repealed in 1859, the bonfires and fireworks are still a feature of Britain's traditional calendar and in Sussex, they are taken rather more seriously. Always the occasion for the odd riot or demonstration, the people of Lewes took things too far in 1847, attacked a local magistrate's house and had The Riot Act read to them. As a result, to meet the authorities halfway, Bonfire Societies were set up, who organised the festivities in various parts of the town. There are six societies today, with their own 'livery' of colourful striped jerseys and caps, while each society's Pioneers wear full costume as monks, Red Indians or Vikings. Burning, paraffin soaked, torches are carried through the streets, along with 'No Popery' or patriotic Union Jack banners.

Rousing national songs like 'Rule Britannia', and 'Pack Up Your Troubles' accompany the revellers to the bonfires, where effigies, usually of the year's most hated politicians are ceremonially burnt, accompanied by a riot of bangers and Roman Candles. This year the Cliffe Society chose instead to make a 'Hard Times' tableau with 23 times larger than life sized hand, tipping up an empty purse. The whole thing, peppered with many fireworks went up in a blaze of flame and coloured sparks to rival any giant bonfire.

113

Nov 12th-18th 1974

IN THE NEWS

Tuesday 12 — **"Thames Salmon"** The first salmon since 1833 has been found in the River Thames which, until recent efforts to clean it up, was so polluted it could not support marine life.

Wednesday 13 — **"Eggs Thrown"** Three eggs were thrown from the crowd as the Queen left by car after touring the Halifax Building Society HQ in West Yorkshire. One hit the pavement, another hit the car and an equerry was splashed.

Thursday 14 — **"Thunderstorms and Gales"** Heavy rain left a trail of damage and flooding across Britain. The huge Union Jack flying over the Houses of Parliament was torn to a quarter of its full size and had to be replaced.

Friday 15 — **"Heating for Old"** New heating allowances are hoped to encourage the elderly to use their central heating. Until now, £1.60 was regarded as a 'reasonable amount' to spend per week on heating, but now, a 'local' average figure will be taken, and the difference made up in allowances.

Saturday 16 — **"Creative Art as Elixir"** Doctors specialising in geriatric treatment have found that creative arts and crafts can give patients a new interest in life and a 'sense of identity through achievement'.

Sunday 17 — **"Yugoslavs Free Britons"** Two British plane spotters who were jailed for alleged espionage, have been freed by the Yugoslav authorities. They were arrested last October outside a military airport and sentenced to four years' imprisonment.

Monday 18 — **"Pledge to The Hungry"** The world food conference last week in Rome ended with the nations pledging to ensure that *'within a decade no child will go to bed hungry, that no family will fear for its next day's bread'*.

HERE IN BRITAIN

"Primate's Auction"

An unusual auction sale will be held by the Archbishop of Canterbury, who is moving to a small cottage in Oxfordshire when he retires after 13 years in office. Five hundred lots cover a wide range of gifts, household items, antiques, furniture, paintings and ecclesiastical ephemera which is all too much for his new property.

There was a viewing day this week and the public, mostly middle-aged women, grasped the opportunity to poke round the Palace where most of the rooms were open, and the furniture and other household goods neatly laid out for inspection.

AROUND THE WORLD

"Iron Maid of Nuremberg"

One of the cruellest instruments for execution ever devised, is up for auction in Berne. It is from the collection of the late Adrian Conan Doyle, son of Sir Arthur, the author, who once described it as 'the most infamous woman in history'.

The 'Iron Maid', from Germany, looks like a woman wearing a cloak stretching to the ground, and is hinged in front so that the victim can be placed inside, with knives mounted on the inside of the door pointing inwards. Then the door, controlled by a clockwork mechanism, closes slowly.

Beaujolais Nouveau

This British charity event was hatched on the 18th November, 1970 over a dinner of coq au vin in the hotel Maritonnes, shared by friends Clement Freud and Joseph Berkmann. Owner of eight London restaurants, Berkmann also ran a wine distribution company and wrote a weekly column for The Sunday Times. Clement Freud was Director of the London Playboy Club, a Liberal MP and wine correspondent for The Sun.

Over several bottles of wine that evening, this jolly wheeze of an idea took shape and sometime after midnight, they roared away from Romanèche in France, with several cases of Beaujolais in the back of each car, having challenged each other to be the first to get their cases back to London. For two years the race was a private event between them, with Berkmann winning both times and much joshing took place in their respective columns, until eventually, word got around that something interesting was going on, and 'The Beaujolais Race' was begun. In 1973, Sunday Times columnist, Alan Hall, delivered the challenge to 'Bring Back the Beaujolais', offering a bottle of Champagne for the first team to deliver a bottle of the new vintage to his desk.

The winner this year was John Patterson, the owner of 'Tiles Restaurant' in London, plonking a case of 1974 Beaujolais Primeur on Hall's desk at 2.30 am, just three and a half hours after leaving Burgundy. He flew the wine over in a Cessna 310 light aircraft to Gatwick, winning by only a few seconds because he was lucky enough to find the front door of The Sunday Times open for the cleaners. The runners-up, Peter Dominic's Wine Mine Club, also used a Cessna 310, but landed at Heathrow and used the newspaper's back door.

Nov 19th - 25th 1974

IN THE NEWS

Tuesday 19 — **"Bupa First"** Bupa which provides private medical treatment has opened its first hospital, with 58 beds and an operating theatre, for subscribers to its insurance scheme.

Wednesday 20 — **"Victory in Sight"** The world is very close to realising "a public health miracle" in the total eradication of smallpox, according to the World Health Organisation. A minimum of £1m is needed to complete the eradication campaign.

Thursday 21 — **"MP Feared Drowned"** John Stonehouse, Labour MP for Walsall, is feared drowned in Miami. He was last seen going swimming, and his clothes were found in a beach side changing room.

Friday 22 — **"Birmingham Pub Bombs"** A call from a man with an Irish accent warned bombs had been planted in two pubs and despite police efforts, the explosions took place within 12 minutes. 19 people were killed and taxis and cars took the injured to hospital.

Saturday 23 — **"New Laws"** In the aftermath of the Birmingham bombings, emergency legislation is to be brought in to combat terrorism. The Bill will extend the length of time police can hold people without charge, give new powers to immigration authorities to turn back unwanted Irishmen and extend the law relating to deportations.

Sunday 24 — **"Oxford Equality"** Female students at Oxford have started a campaign to have equal numbers of men and women students and dons admitted. Their campaign 'Women Against the Quota', does not allow men at the meetings.

Monday 25 — **"Welsh Language TV Gets Home Secretary's Blessing"** The Government has agreed that a television service for Wales, with priority for Welsh language programmes, should be launched as soon as possible.

HERE IN BRITAIN
"Under the Kilt"

Soldiers in Scottish regiments who wear the kilt in the traditional manner, without underclothes, will take part in tests at the Western General Hospital in Edinburgh, to examine a theory that tight underwear may make man less fertile than animals.

Scientists have proved that men produce only 60% viable sperm whereas animals can produce up to 98 %. *"We think this is because animals wear no clothes"* said one doctor at the hospital's Clinical and Population Cytogenetics unit. A study will also be carried out on a primitive Nigerian tribe who wear no clothes.

AROUND THE WORLD
"Imperial Welcome"

The first 'goodwill' visit to Japan by an American President took place amid strikes and violent demonstrations, when Gerald Ford was welcomed by Emperor Hirohito at the Imperial Palace, in central Tokyo.

So tight were the security arrangements that Mr Ford's personal photographer was temporarily arrested when he rushed out of the President's official aircraft wearing blue jeans, to record the historic moment of an American head of state stepping on to Japanese soil. Apologising, the police said they thought *'he looked like a demonstrator'*.

MISS WORLD

'Miss United Kingdom', Helen Morgan, won the 'Miss World' contest at the Albert Hall this month. Miss Morgan won the 'Miss Wales' title in June and has a baby son but has decided to resign her title after only five days because of public criticism of the fact that she is a mother and speculation on her personal life. In her resignation statement, she said she believed that rumours about her might have an undesirable and distressing effect on her son and family. This has presented the organisers of the contest with their second crisis within a year as the previous Miss World resigned after four months, also because of undesirable publicity. 'Miss South Africa' who was the runner-up in the latest contest is now 'Miss World'.

This is all a far cry from Eric Morley's original vision for the first contest back in 1951. Mr. Morley, who was an English show host, and founder of the long running TV favourite 'Come Dancing', founded the beauty pageant as part of the Festival of Britain celebrations, calling it the 'Festival Bikini Contest.' The event was popular with the press, who named it 'Miss World', but from the start there were some objections to the newly introduced bikini, which was considered immodest, so future contests featured girls wearing more modest one-piece swimsuits instead.

The contest was first televised in 1959, and during the 60's it was one of the most watched programmes on television. The 1970 pageant was notable for being interrupted by Women's Libbers armed with water pistols loaded with ink. South Africa added to the controversy that year by entering both a black and a white contestant and the country was then banned from the contest until apartheid was abolished.

Nov 26th - Dec 2nd 1974

IN THE NEWS

Tuesday 26 — **"Two Hearts"** A new technique has been pioneered in South Africa by Professor Christian Barnard, who implanted a second heart in a man's chest without removing the man's own heart.

Wednesday 27 — **"Last Tango Degrading?"** The film, 'Last Tango in Paris' has gone on trial at the Central Criminal Court in the most important obscenity trial since 'Lady Chatterley's Lover' in 1960. The jury, which includes three women, must decide whether the film is obscene.

Thursday 28 — **"Terrorism Bill Passed"** The parliamentary bill proscribes the IRA, making membership an offence and empowers the Home Secretary to expel terrorists from Britain. More MPs are calling for the death penalty for acts of terrorism involving murder.

Friday 29 — **"New Foreign Minister"** Radio Uganda announced that President Idi Amin has taken over the post of foreign minister from Miss Bagaya, whom he dismissed, alleging she had made love to a European in a Paris airport toilet.

Saturday 30 — **"No Hand Signals"** The Minister for Transport has proposed that demonstration of hand signals in the driving test should be dispensed with, but candidates should still be expected to use arm signals for *"I intend to slow down or stop"*.

Sunday 1 — **"Sunday Ban"** A shortage of sliced bread is expected next week when a ban on overtime and Sunday work begins. 280 bakeries, making three quarters of the country's bread including Sunblest, Mother's Pride, Homepride and Wonderloaf, are closed.

Monday 2 — **"Deep Freeze Sheep"** Sheep rustling in Scotland is increasing, with Argyllshire worst affected. The National Farmers' Union are asking chief constables for more protection and blame increased purchases of deep freezers for the rise in thefts.

HERE IN BRITAIN
"Colonel In 'Bottom-Spanking' Case"

A 64-year-old Lieutenant-Colonel has won his 'bottom-spanking' libel action against the Sunday People, who accused him of trapping young girls for sexual purposes. The jury of nine men and three women took three hours to find the former mayor and solicitor had been libelled but awarded only 2p damages, leaving each side to pay their own cost.

Afterwards he said he would continue to spank *'pretty, willing and tempting girls. As far as I am concerned, we won.'* Nearby workmen on scaffolding, on being told the result shouted, *'We'll have a collection for you!'*

AROUND THE WORLD
"Spacecraft Will Send Jupiter Close-Ups"

Pioneer 11, the second terrestrial visitor to Jupiter, will pass 26,613 miles above the planet's surface this week, much closer than Pioneer 10. NASA officials are hoping that the spacecraft will survive the very high radiation from the planet as it will spend about 30 minutes in the most intense part of the radiation belt, with most of the instruments shut down. Immediately afterwards it will be apparent whether the rest of its mission can be completed. It should send back close-up pictures of Jupiter's south pole and the 'Great Red Spot' before its moment of closest approach.

Remembering Coco

Midgets, strong men, tight rope walkers, trapeze artists and the whole family of the English circus met beneath the biggest top in London, St Paul's, to remember Coco the Clown this week. The Dean conducted a memorial service, with children's hymns and the Russian Kontakion of the Departed, for Nikolai Poliakov, the poor boy from Latvia.

Nikolai's family worked at the local theatre to supplement the money his father earned as a cobbler and five-year-old Nikolai started singing for food to avoid starvation. He ran away in 1908 to join a circus in Belarus and spent the next 21 years perfecting his character with various Soviet circuses. He was nicknamed Kokishka or 'little cat' which eventually became Coco when he first came to Britain in 1929. His trademark costume of size 58 boots, big baggy pants and bright red hair that stood on end at unexpected moments, was that of an 'Auguste', the foolish one always getting the buckets of water and custard pies from the 'Clown', who is the smart guy with a sad white face, conical hat and harlequin costume.

The Mills brothers, whose circus Coco belonged to from the 1930s, were at the service and so was 'Mrs Coco,' and many of the children who felt they were personal friends of the man whose domed eyebrows made him seem permanently surprised. His passion for children was mutual. He would put on his make-up and costume after breakfast and visit children's wards in hospitals between performances. The thousands of children who were saved from death or mutilation by his continual campaigning for road safety are his living memorials and so are 'the millions who laughed with him and loved him.' He was the 'brilliant star that brightened up our lives for over 30 years.'

DEC 3RD – DEC 9TH 1974

IN THE NEWS

Tuesday 3 — **"NSPCC Calls for Aid"** The National Society for the Prevention of Cruelty to Children are seeking Government help as rising costs have adversely affected them. They predict a £225,000 loss in 1975.

Wednesday 4 — **"Greasy Spoons"** A 'Survey of Toilet and Washing Facilities in England' published this week paints details of dirty bathrooms, broken flushes and poor hand washing facilities. Cafes weren't named, but the roads on which they are located are detailed.

Thursday 5 — **"Monty Python's Flying Circus"** The satirical comedy, famous for the Dead Parrot sketch and Ministry of Silly Walks, has finished, as John Cleese, Eric Idle, Michael Palin, Terry Gilliam, and Grahame Chapman begin to pursue their separate careers.

Friday 6 — **"Royal High Jinks"** Prince Andrew is under observation in hospital following a minor head injury, sustained during a scuffle in his Gordonstoun dormitory. The housemaster commented, *"One cannot stop young schoolboys from larking about."*

Saturday 7 — **"The Show Must Go On"** In Carlisle, a performance of 'The Castaway', based on the life of poet and recluse William Cowper, was more realistic than envisaged as on the opening night not one person went to watch it. In true theatrical tradition the actor carried on in front of 225 empty seats and two usherettes.

Sunday 8 " **Drive Against Marxist Teachers"** A 'National Campaign for Discipline in Schools' has been launched against Marxist and progressive teachers who are said to be contributing to the breakdown of discipline in schools.

Monday 9 — **"Greece Celebrates Decisive Vote to End Monarchy"** Crowds of jubilant people filled the centre of Athens to celebrate the end of the Greek monarchy, and to welcome in the Republic.

HERE IN BRITAIN

"Do-It-Yourself Messiah"

Handel's Oratorio 'The Messiah' is very popular and a performance in the Albert Hall this week was certainly innovative. Members of the public who have always wanted to perform there, were invited to do just that. Unrehearsed, a handful of professionals were joined by 250 amateur musicians, along with a 2,000 strong choir, many of whom had only sung before in the bath. There may have been a few more hallelujahs than Handel intended, but as one person commented, *"It was a courageous venture and a wonderful sound.*

AROUND THE WORLD

"Chinese Highway Code"

Traffic police managed to calm Peking's normally chaotic flow of bicycles and pedestrians, where the expansion of the city's diplomatic community has been marked by a great increase in accidents involving diplomat driven cars. Government policy in the case of a fatality, is to expel the diplomat with a fine of £2,000. This has caused much bitterness on the part of the foreigners, who consider it to be irrational, whilst at the same time, there is a good deal of resentment among the Chinese about the number of foreigners who drive too fast.

BREAD ON THE RISE

The nation's housewives have been taking steps to ensure that the recent bread shortages won't catch them out. The Health Food Manufacturers' Association said that the demand for strong bread flour and yeast increased five-fold this week, whilst the director of Boots the Chemists, said his company had recorded a great increase in the sales of yeast. The Flour Advisory Bureau helpfully published a recipe for an emergency cob loaf without yeast, but with the proviso that the *"resulting object is best eaten fresh, hot from the oven"* as it would probably be hard as rock the next day. This is remarkably similar to the first bread made by Neolithic bakers 12,000 years ago, when coarsely crushed grain was mixed with water and the resultant dough, baked on hot stones covered with ashes. Now, purists among home bakers will go to great lengths to obtain stone ground flour, but professional millers are sceptical about claims that bread made from 'pure' ingredients is healthier and tastes nuttier.

The first mechanical dough-mixer, invented by a Greek slave under the Roman Empire, comprised donkeys walking in circles round a large stone basin pulling paddles in the mixture, producing enough dough to make hundreds of loaves. Without a mixer, even a kitchen sized one, most housewives knead dough by hand. Mrs Audrey Ellison, a master home baker said, *"Home baking is a therapeutic craft, and the act of kneading is physically and psychologically soothing."* The only downside in baking one's own bread is the wonderful aroma, which makes the family eat more bread, reducing any savings in the housekeeping money. Until recently, home baking, was considered an almost magical art because of the need to regenerate and ferment your own yeast but the advent of dried yeast has made it easier.

Dec 10th - Dec 16th 1974

IN THE NEWS

Tuesday 10 — **"Own Planes Shot Down"** More than 60 NATO aircraft were "shot down" by their own side in a naval exercise because they were using different systems of communication.

Wednesday 11 — **"Veteran Submarine"** Last of the Royal Navy submarines designed to fight in World War II, the HMS Andrew, visited the Pool of London yesterday before being broken up.

Thursday 12 — **"Jane Austen Stamps"** To commemorate her bicentenary, the first woman author to be shown on British stamps is to be Jane Austen, along with characters from her books.

Friday 13 — **"Prince of Wales Qualifies"** The Prince of Wales completed his helicopter training at Royal Naval Air Station, Yeovilton. In a fly-past to mark the tenth anniversary of 707 Squadron, he led a formation of 16 helicopters trailing coloured smoke.

Saturday 14 — **"Food Gifts"** Seasonal gifts of sugar, tea, coffee, biscuits and other groceries, donated by big chain supermarkets, were distributed to pensioners in Derby yesterday by the National Housewives Association, which is a network of local groups for women across Great Britain.

Sunday 15 — **"TV Watch on Hooligans"** Closed-circuit TV is to be installed at four London Underground stations to deal with hooligans. The £200,000 system will enable platforms and booking halls to be monitored and enable early police intervention.

Monday 16 — **"Drivers Observe New Limits"** Nine out of ten motorists are obeying the newly introduced fuel-saving speed limits. The new restrictions are 60 mph on dual carriageways and 50 mph on other major roads where there is no lower limit. The motorway limit remains at 70 mph.

HERE IN BRITAIN

"Old Masters in Attics"

Since 'Going For A Song' became popular on TV in 1965 - people have become interested in what is stored away at the back of cupboards or the loft. East Anglia is the birthplace of John Constable and Thomas Gainsborough, and it was to Gainsborough's House in Sudbury that a stream of people came with their treasures wrapped carefully in newspapers and blankets this week in the hope of discovering a hidden fortune.

More than 60 paintings were brought to the house but unfortunately, it turned out there were no Constables or Gainsboroughs among them.

AROUND THE WORLD

"The Fat One"

The Spanish Government have put another 65,000 tickets for their annual lottery on sale at £76 each and boosted the festive prize money to a record breaking £73m. The Christmas lottery, called "El Gordo" ("the fat one"), is scheduled for December 21.

This year it offers 224,889 cash prizes, including 21 prizes worth £572,000 each, and all tax-free. Many Spaniards buy a 'decrino' or fractional ticket representing one-tenth for £7.60, which entitles the owner to one-tenth of any prize money won by the whole number to which the decrino corresponds. *'Feliz Navidad'* everyone!

GHOSTS AND GHOULS

The British fascination with ghostly tales around Christmas time goes back thousands of years and is rooted in ancient celebrations of the winter solstice. In the depths of winter, pagan traditions included a belief in a ghostly procession of riders across the sky, known as The Wild Hunt. Recounting stories of heroism against monstrous and supernatural beings became a midwinter tradition, with dark tales used to entertain on dark nights. Ghosts have been associated with winter cold ever since those ancient times, the 'Ode of Beowulf' being one of the oldest ghost stories, from about the 8th century, about a Scandinavian prince who fights the evil and terrifying monster Grendel. In 1611, Shakespeare wrote 'The Winter's Tale' which includes the line: *"A sad tale's best for winter, I have one of sprites and goblins."*

Almost 200 years later, Mary Shelley set her horror novel 'Frankenstein' in a snowy wasteland. The Victorians made the winter ghost story their own, with the idea of something dreadful lurking beyond the light and laughter, inspiring some famous chilling tales. Elizabeth Gaskell's 'The Old Nurse's Story', Wilkie Collin's 'The Haunted Hotel' and of course the classic Christmas tale of hauntings by Charles Dickens, 'A Christmas Carol' are some of the better-known titles from this period. Many traditional ghost stories are introduced using the literary device of a group of friends telling stories around a roaring fire rather like pagan storytellers around the midwinter fire. Now times have changed, and the central heating has replaced the roaring fire, but we still have a fear of the unknown, a yearning for what is lost and a desire to be secure, and paradoxically we still enjoy the jolt of fear and dread such stories convey, that make the Christmas lights glitter even more brightly.

Dec 17th – Dec 23rd 1974

IN THE NEWS

Tuesday 17 — **"Overseas Doctors"** The Chief Medical Officer has warned more doctors from abroad will have to be employed in the health services if the increased annual demand remains at the 3% level of the past few years.

Wednesday 18 — **"Foreign Office Facade Stays"** The Foreign and Commonwealth Office in Whitehall, is being partially rebuilt, but the Department for the Environment confirms the façade and many interiors will be preserved.

Thursday 19 — **"Census in 1976"** It has been announced that the census will be taken every five years from 1976. It takes 18 months to print the 20 million forms, and recruit 100,000 staff.

Friday 20 — **"Queen's Farmhouse"** While Sandringham is undergoing rebuilding work, the Queen and her family will spend Christmas in a six-bedroom farmhouse on the Sandringham Estate.

Saturday 21 — **"Peking Zoo Gets Two Rhinos"** Two rhinoceroses, Mungo and Nykasi, have been given to Peking Zoo. This is a reciprocal gift from London Zoo for the two pandas sent to Britain after Mr Heath's visit to China this year.

Sunday 22 — **"Heath's Home Bombed"** A bomb was thrown on to a balcony ten minutes before Mr Heath arrived at his home in Belgravia, last night. Windows were shattered but house staff were unhurt. A car believed to have been used in the raid was later found abandoned.

Monday 23 — **"Buy Tickets-On-Board"** British Airways is launching the first scheduled shuttle service in Europe, where passengers will pay on board the aircraft. The service will link London and Glasgow, which yearly carries 600,000 passengers. There will also be free of charge refreshments in the departure lounge.

HERE IN BRITAIN

"Battle Lines Redrawn At Naseby"

There are plans to build a road link costing £9m-£15m between the A1 and M1 to carry traffic from the East Anglian ports. It will skirt Naseby's battlefield, where Cromwell gained victory in 1645, by a whisker. There are two options for the route, both of which spell environmental disaster for either Haselbech or Naseby, depending on which option is taken.

Both village Parish Councils are set to object to the plans, and both are determined they will win. The sub-post-master of Naseby said, *"If this continues there will be another battle of Naseby!"*

AROUND THE WORLD

"Zaire Expedition"

A British led international expedition which set out in early October to explore the river Zaire in Africa, arrived at Kinshasa after a journey of 73 days and more than 2,000 miles. The team of 40 have followed the river's 2,718-mile course using long rubber dinghies built to tackle the river's dangerous rapids.

The last phase of the journey, from Kinshasa to the river mouth, will begin in early January. The river party has been backed up by a shore group of 100, which includes doctors, zoologists and botanists, who are studying tropical diseases.

CHRISTMAS COINS

Once upon a time there were always new pennies for Christmas. Public spending reached its peak in December and all available coin was required for the nation's pocket money and that is why new money usually made its appearance at this season. Minting was suspended during the war to save copper for munitions, but to make up for the deficit, large quantities of pennies were struck between 1944 and 1948 after which the Mint not only ceased striking pennies but withdrew some from circulation. In 1950 and 51 only token quantities of pennies were struck for the special specimen sets that proved so popular, but for many households still suffering the bleak aftermath of the war years, a few pennies saved from the housekeeping which found their way into the toe of a Christmas stocking had to do.

As Britain's prosperity slowly recovered in the late 50's and early 60's, the stocking might be blessed with a 'tanner' or a 'bob' (a sixpence piece or a shilling), and if you were very lucky a shiny half-crown might be nestled among the tangerines and novelties. Sadly, everything seemed to change after February 1971, and the magic of Christmas Pennies faded with the appearance of its much smaller cousin - the gaudy copper 1p coin - which could slip away through the holes in a Christmas stocking without anyone really noticing. Not so the shiny sixpence, which entered Christmas tradition, courtesy of Queen Victoria's husband, Prince Albert, who introduced the custom of putting a silver sixpence in the pudding mix on the 1st Sunday of Advent. All the family had a stir and made a wish. On Christmas Day whoever found the coin in their portion of dessert was assured of wealth and good luck in the year to come.

125

Dec 24th – Dec 31st 1974

IN THE NEWS

Tuesday 24   **"Dartmoor Carols Cancelled"** Striking Prison officers at Dartmoor prison means the carol concert has been cancelled, but the film, 'The Great Train Robbery,' was shown.

Wednesday 25   **"The Pope Opens Holy Year"** The Pope opened the Roman Catholic Holy Year and the Christmas celebrations just before midnight on Christmas Eve with three blows from an ornamental silver hammer on the "holy door" into St Peter's Basilica.

Thursday 26   **"Airborne Evacuation of Darwin"** Following a cyclone on Christmas Day, a fleet of planes has been flying the sick and injured out of Darwin in North Australia.

Friday 27   **"Warmest Christmas"** The Christmas period was the warmest since records began at the London Weather Centre in 1940, with the highest ever recorded Christmas Day temperature of 15 degrees centigrade.

Saturday 28   **"More Royal Shoots"** One of the heaviest pheasant shooting programmes ever held at Sandringham has been arranged. Next week there will be five shoots and during the rest of January there will be three shoots a week.

Sunday 29   **"Shells Fired Near Scots Trawler"** After a failed 10-hour chase across the North Sea by a Danish gunboat, a Scottish trawler has been accused of breaching fishing limits and will be taken to court.

Monday 30   **"Christmas Refuge"** Over 500 homeless people spent the Christmas in the stark but warm interior of a disused church by Lambeth Palace, organised by Crisis at Christmas.

Tuesday 31   **"Monarchy Loses Last Powers"** King Carl XVI Gustaf of Sweden presided over a Cabinet meeting today for the last time.

HERE IN BRITAIN

"Boxing Day"

The 26th of December is the Feast of St. Stephen, who was a deacon of the earliest church, chosen by Jesus' disciples to look after the poor and widows, and hence poor, or alms, boxes were opened in church and distributed on this day. Later in the Middle Ages, it became the custom to give small gifts of food or money to servants for their loyalty and hard work.

This evolved into the practice of tradesmen such as the coalman, milkman or greengrocer calling at their customers' houses for their 'Christmas Box' or bonus money.

AROUND THE WORLD

"Breakfast with the President"

Four Paris road sweepers were invited by President Giscard D'Estaing to have breakfast with him at the Elysée Palace on Christmas Eve. The dustmen, from Mali and Senegal, with their French foreman, were sweeping the streets outside the Elysée when he called them in for coffee, rolls, and croissants and a 20-minute chat. Afterwards they each received a Christmas present of a turkey and a bottle of champagne. The Public Services' Union commented sourly *"the President would have done better to have intervened more quickly during the dustmen's strike last month."*

THE TRAFALGAR TREE

Norway's annual gift of a Christmas tree is in pride of place at Trafalgar Square. The 63-foot, four ton, tree, is one of the most impressive yet, and thousands of people flocked to London on Saturday 14th to watch the Norwegian Ambassador ceremoniously switch the tree lights on, and will remains lit until January 6, better known as the twelfth night .

The first tree was sent from Oslo in 1947 as a token of gratitude to the British people for their help during the second world war when Great Britain was Norway's closest ally. London was where the Norwegian King Haakon VII and his government fled as their country was occupied, and it was from here that much of Norway's resistance movement was organised. Both the BBC and its Norwegian counterpart NRK would broadcast in Norwegian from London, something that was both an important source of information and a boost of morale for those who remained in Norway, where people would listen in secret to their forbidden radios. The idea to send a pine to Britain was first conceived by the Norwegian naval commando, Mons Urangsvå, who sent a tree from the island of Hisøy which had been cut down during a raid to London in 1942 as a gift to King Haakon and King George V decided that it should be installed in Trafalgar Square where it stood *'evergreen with defiant hope'*.

The trees come from the snow-covered forest area surrounding Oslo, known as "Oslomarka", an area populated with moose, lynx, roe deer, and even the odd wolf, and legions of pine trees. A worthy tree is located by the head forester and space is cleared around it to allow light from all angles, and it is tended through the years to secure optimal growth.

1974 Calendar

January
S	M	T	W	T	F	S
		1	2	3	4	5
6	7	8	9	10	11	12
13	14	15	16	17	18	19
20	21	22	23	24	25	26
27	28	29	30	31		

February
S	M	T	W	T	F	S
					1	2
3	4	5	6	7	8	9
10	11	12	13	14	15	16
17	18	19	20	21	22	23
24	25	26	27	28		

March
S	M	T	W	T	F	S
					1	2
3	4	5	6	7	8	9
10	11	12	13	14	15	16
17	18	19	20	21	22	23
24	25	26	27	28	29	30
31						

April
S	M	T	W	T	F	S
	1	2	3	4	5	6
7	8	9	10	11	12	13
14	15	16	17	18	19	20
21	22	23	24	25	26	27
28	29	30				

May
S	M	T	W	T	F	S
			1	2	3	4
5	6	7	8	9	10	11
12	13	14	15	16	17	18
19	20	21	22	23	24	25
26	27	28	29	30	31	

June
S	M	T	W	T	F	S
						1
2	3	4	5	6	7	8
9	10	11	12	13	14	15
16	17	18	19	20	21	22
23	24	25	26	27	28	29
30						

July
S	M	T	W	T	F	S
	1	2	3	4	5	6
7	8	9	10	11	12	13
14	15	16	17	18	19	20
21	22	23	24	25	26	27
28	29	30	31			

August
S	M	T	W	T	F	S
				1	2	3
4	5	6	7	8	9	10
11	12	13	14	15	16	17
18	19	20	21	22	23	24
25	26	27	28	29	30	31

September
S	M	T	W	T	F	S
1	2	3	4	5	6	7
8	9	10	11	12	13	14
15	16	17	18	19	20	21
22	23	24	25	26	27	28
29	30					

October
S	M	T	W	T	F	S
		1	2	3	4	5
6	7	8	9	10	11	12
13	14	15	16	17	18	19
20	21	22	23	24	25	26
27	28	29	30	31		

November
S	M	T	W	T	F	S
					1	2
3	4	5	6	7	8	9
10	11	12	13	14	15	16
17	18	19	20	21	22	23
24	25	26	27	28	29	30

December
S	M	T	W	T	F	S
1	2	3	4	5	6	7
8	9	10	11	12	13	14
15	16	17	18	19	20	21
22	23	24	25	26	27	28
29	30	31				

Printed in Great Britain
by Amazon

257225e3-7529-42a0-90d5-920dd425eea1R01